ABOUT THE AUTHOR

Alex Quick is the author of *102 Free Things to Do*, *102 Ways to Write a Novel* and *102 English Things to Do*. This book is the fruit of Alex's experience, or lack of experience, or both.

102 WAYS
TO
IMPROVE
YOUR
PARTNER

First published in 2013 by Old Street Publishing Ltd,
Trebinshun House, Brecon LD3 7PX
www.oldstreetpublishing.co.uk

ISBN 978 1 908699 34 3

Copyright in the text © Alex Quick, 2013
Copyright in the illustrations © James Nunn, 2013

The right of Alex Quick to be identified as the author of this work has been asserted by him in
accordance with the Copyright, Designs and Patents Act 1988.

Every effort has been made obtain permission for all illustrations, but in the event of an
omission the publisher should be contacted.

All rights reserved. No part of this publication may be reproduced, stored in or introduced
into a retrieval system, or transmitted, in any form, or by any means (electronic, mechanical,
photocopying, recording or otherwise) without the prior written permission of the publisher.

10 9 8 7 6 5 4 3 2 1

A CIP catalogue record for this title is available from the British Library.

Printed and bound in Great Britain

To Carole, Clement and Isambard

102 WAYS

TO

IMPROVE

YOUR

PARTNER

ALEX QUICK

CONTENTS

1.

YOUR PARTNER IS ALLERGIC TO CANDLES, ROSES AND RED WINE

Your partner may be allergic to all these things without necessarily being allergic to Romance. An allergy to candles is quite common among asthmatics. Roses or any other strongly scented flowers are difficult for those prone to rhinitis or hayfever. Many people react badly to the tannins in red grapes.

The problem, if you deduce from this that your partner is Unromantic, lies in your somewhat restricted idea of Romance. True Romantics cast their net much wider. Places and situations redolent of Romance might include: a cinema with worn seats that no one visits; a park where a lonely woman is practising on a flute; a boy learning German on his own because he once met a German girl at a bus station. If you truly desire that your partner become more romantic, enlarge your own ideas about what constitutes Romance, to encompass the vulnerability of human beings lost among vast forces, the memories that inhere ghostlike in ordinary objects, etc.

If you discuss these things with you partner you may find that they feel them just as keenly as you do.

2.

YOUR PARTNER USES THE BUTTER KNIFE IN THE MARMITE JAR

Try the following: as your partner is dipping the butter-smeared knife into the pristine depths of the Marmite jar, give a playful cry of 'Billie!' When your partner looks quizzically at you, say: 'Oh, we used to say that as children. We had a dog called Billie who was mad about Marmite. She'd stand on her hind legs to reach the table and try to lick the jar. Needless to say we had to throw the pot away if she got her tongue in it. We later extended it to anyone who used the butter knife in the Marmite jar. It's just a family tradition.'

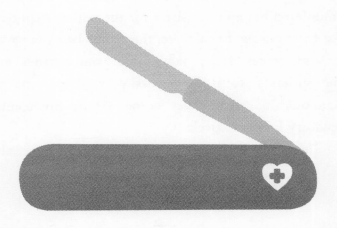

3.

YOUR PARTNER HAS COMMITTED A MURDER

How seriously you should take this entirely depends what sort of murder. If your partner has been on a killing spree and gunned down some shoppers queuing for lottery tickets, that is technically not a murder, but a massacre. If they have killed someone in a war, that is not murder but heroism. If they have killed in self-defence, that is justifiable homicide. Murder, like the truth, is rarely pure and never simple (to quote Oscar Wilde).

Let's say your partner has committed the type of murder that is generally roundly condemned by all. They have broken into an old lady's house and murdered her and her sister for the pathetic contents of their purses. Even there, there may be extenuating circumstances. It's possible that your partner may be suffering from Dostoyevsky Syndrome, or the compulsion to re-enact scenes from nineteenth-century Russian novels.

The fact is that any conceivable crime is forgivable

given detailed enough knowledge of the situation. What do the French say? *Tout comprendre c'est tout pardonner.* 'To understand all is to forgive all.'

Get out the spade and lend a hand.

4.

YOUR PARTNER DOES DIY AND IS RUINING THE HOUSE

Send your partner on a DIY training course. Avert the sense that this is a criticism by sending them on an 'Advanced' course, despite the fact that they are not in any sense 'Advanced'. Have a word with the tutor beforehand and explain the situation.

This will both resolve the issue and create a genuinely skilled handyperson for your household needs.

5.

YOUR PARTNER LEAVES THE LAVATORY SEAT UP/DOWN

If your partner habitually leaves the lavatory seat up, it is likely that they are a) a man who is decent enough to raise the seat but is not quite decent enough to lower it afterwards, b) a woman who raises the seat afterwards to prepare the lavatory for the next user who she anticipates will be a male, or c) a woman who urinates standing[1]. If your partner habitually leaves the lavatory seat *down* it is likely that they are a) a man who is considerate of the feelings of his womenfolk, b) a man who is not at all considerate of the feelings of his womenfolk and never bothers raising the seat in the first place, c) a woman who assumes the next user of the lavatory will be a woman, d) a woman who does not know who the next user of the lavatory will be but considers the default position of the seat to be properly down, e) a woman of the Ellis type who is particularly careless, f) a woman who knows that the

---

1 I hesitate to mention c) here, but it is a phenomenon well attested in *Studies in the Psychology of Sex*, vol. 3 (1896) by Havelock Ellis.

next user of the lavatory will be male but wishes to make life difficult for them, or g) a man or a woman in a household where both sexes sit. Possibilities for h), i), j), k) and l) immediately suggest themselves, but space is limited. Suffice it to say that this is an enormously complex area and no solution can be offered without knowing all the facts of the case. All I can do here is to refer readers to the forthcoming Improvers Pamphlet §102LS1(iv) due for release some time in the late Spring.

6.

YOUR PARTNER LOVES DOGS

A dog-loving partner needn't be a problem. However, if you shudder at the very thought of dogs, and regard them as smelly, unhygienic, expensive, bothersome, flea-ridden monsters, then a dog-loving partner may be regarded as in need of substantial improvement.

I admit that I personally abhor dogs. I abhor their waste products. I abhor the idea of following them around with a little plastic bag. I abhor seeing said little plastic bags hanging on railings near where I live, as if the dog-owner, having chosen to be responsible, had suddenly suffered a moral *bouleversement* and decided to advertise the fact.

How to deal with a dog-loving partner in these circumstances? Well, the partner must be gently brought over to the light. They must be made to see that dogs are frankly disgusting. A good way to achieve this is to list all the diseases that dogs can bring into the home. These include hookworm, roundworm, tapeworm, heartworm, rabies, septicaemia, campylobacteriosis, tick-borne encephalitis, Lyme disease, leishmaniasis and babesiosis. Most of these diseases are contracted through eating something contaminated by faeces from dog stools, a not uncommon occurrence in a dog-owning household. Live with a dog for long, and you will find yourself quite literally eating its excrement.

Our dogs give us a great deal of love and unconditional loyalty. They also give us blindness, diarrhoea, abdominal pain, inflammation of the digestive tract, severe itching, collapse of the dermis, vomiting, fever and death.

Present this information in a spirit of gentle concern.

7.

YOUR PARTNER IS ADDICTED TO SELF-HELP BOOKS

Self-help books are, it goes without saying, the scourge of the age. Nothing is more calculated to ruin the peace of a happy home than a partner who tries to Change their Life for the Better.

Books on relationships can be especially damaging. The secret of dealing with a partner who is given to perusing books with titles such as *Why You Are Wounded* or *Servants of the Sacred Feminine* is simple: you must take these idiocies as seriously as your partner does. This is the principle of the Mirroring of Undesirable Traits (MUT). The idea is to reflect the dicta of the self-help gurus back to your partner, only translated into normal English so as to make those mantras seem ridiculous. So, for example, the term 'passive-aggressive'.[2] Adopt a look of effortful mystification involving a slight drawing-in of the jaw and say slowly: 'So, if I've got it right, "passive-aggressive" behaviour is any disagreement that doesn't involve actual hitting.'

---

2 You will inevitably, at some point, be accused of being 'passive-aggressive'.

Business and management self-help books are another area in which MUT can be applied to good effect. Begin leaving your own self-help books around the home: if you can, get a copy of Steven F. Whitewhine's classic *The Tao of HR: How the Teachings of Lao-Tzu Transformed a FTSE 100 Company* and leave it on the dining-room table. Allied to MUT is the principle of Go One Further (GOF): so for example, if your partner is considering ways of downsizing the family business to make it leaner and fitter, the GOF-practitioner will in all seriousness suggest destroying it entirely. 'You know' (you should say), 'I sometimes feel that we've got so hung up on *adding* value, *adding* expertise, we've forgotten about taking them away. I mean, what do you get if you strip a company of what is conventionally considered its assets? Just a desk and a telephone? But how did most successful companies start? Precisely like that!'

For a partner who is addicted to more conventional self-help books, such as DIY manuals, there is really nothing to improve, since it is useful to have a partner who is willing to do difficult jobs such as replacing guttering on high ladders or re-grouting splash-backs. However, for a partner who believes they are more capable in this area than they actually are, Improvers should refer again to §4.

8.

YOUR PARTNER IS A MALINGERER

Nowadays there is much talk of 'man flu', despite the fact that women visit the doctor 1.4 times as much as men do and are 1.6 times as likely to take time off work, rising to 4.8 during the men's singles finals at Wimbledon. But the truth is that both sexes are equally likely to malinger. What is needed is practical help.

The first approach is to suggest to an ailing or pseudo-ailing partner that they have over-diagnosed their own illness. To a partner who clutches their temples and says, 'I would come to the christening, if it weren't for this migraine,' say: 'Is the pain unilateral?' If they then reply: 'Well, it's only me who's got it,' say: 'I mean does it affect only one side? And is it accompanied both by optical sensitivity and vomiting? Because otherwise it's unlikely to be a classic migraine.' This is likely to be met with a sullen silence.

Another approach is to suggest that you have what they have, only worse. To anyone who claims pain in the joints, for example, say: 'I know just what you mean. It's awful, isn't it. Here, try a Bromazedam. They always get me through.'

If neither of these gambits work, try leaving all the windows open, even in winter, to give the patient fresh air. Or arrange for relatives to visit, as if your partner really is at death's door. Soon your partner will find that being sick is much more uncomfortable and embarrassing than simply being well, and will pull themselves together.

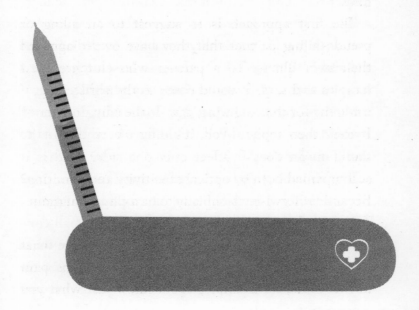

9.

YOUR PARTNER INTERRUPTS YOU IN THE MIDDLE OF YOUR SENTENCE BY BRUSHING IMAGINARY DANDRUFF FROM YOUR SHOULDER

Or conceivably real dandruff. Fix your partner with a gimlet stare and say: 'I put that dandruff there deliberately. It's actually grated Parmesan cheese. I've come to realise that I am irresistibly attractive to the opposite sex and I want to do something to lessen the effect I have on them, while maintaining my generally impeccable dress, by introducing this small unhygienic note. I would have thought you would have been the first to thank me for this.'

This will obviously be untrue but it will cow your partner and they will hesitate before interrupting you again

You could go to the lengths of having a small container of Parmesan about your person to show them as you say this, but this would presuppose that you really are sprinkling cheese on yourself, which I presume you are not.

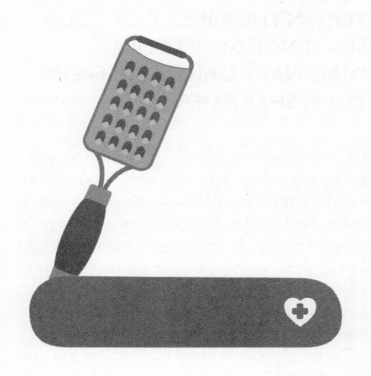

10.

YOUR PARTNER OVERUSES THE WORD 'FUNKY'

Dealing with a vocabulary-related offence can be very ticklish, but if the offence revolves about a word such as 'funky', or centres on text-speak such as 'brb' (actually spelled out in conversation), or on any other word derived from popular culture and probably a decade or more out of date, action *must* be taken.

First, attempt an account of the word's origins. 'Now that's an interesting word,' you might say. 'I found out the other day that it comes from 1920s New Orleans. Apparently it means [insert some explicit reference here]. But of course no one realises that these days. Amazing that were actually going round saying this all day long.'

If this fails to work, mention a media personality whom your partner loathes, and in the midst of a thoroughgoing assault on his or her looks, personal morality and *Weltanschaung*, say: 'And the worst thing is that they are always using that word [insert word here]. I can't stand that. It makes them sound like Tony Blair circa 1998.'

11.

YOUR PARTNER DOESN'T LISTEN TO YOU

The American psychologist Stanley Milgram carried out some experiments in the 1960s in which spouses were encouraged by a white-coated figure to give electric shocks of increasing severity to their own partners, up to and including a shock labelled 'Danger of death'. To his consternation, Milgram found that spouses proceeded immediately to the most lethal surge when their life-mate failed to respond appropriately to simple remarks such as 'Have you seen my glasses?', 'Melissa was acting up at work today' and 'Well, one of us has to attend the parents' evening.'

What to do? Well, it is possible that the problem is that you don't say anything worth hearing. You may have been saying the same things since 1971. Your partner knows your opinions on everything from Jamie Oliver to chemical castration (or perhaps both at the same time). The solution is never to say anything in your partner's presence that you've ever said before.

The degree of difficulty you experience with this will give you an idea of the degree to which the problem is your own fault.

However, it may be that you simply bore your partner. This is not necessarily a bad thing. See §47.

12.

YOUR PARTNER ERUCTATES UNAPOLOGETICALLY

It has long been noted that hydrogen sulphide and personal chemistry do not mix. For that reason, it is very rare that a partner will introduce this particular form of behaviour into the early stages of a relationship. Yet, the human body being what it is, it may make its appearance not long after the first kiss, if not simultaneously with it.

Remarks such as 'Is there a draught?', 'The natives are getting restless', or 'There's a breathless hush in the Close tonight' may fall on deaf ears. Developing the habit yourself will only encourage your partner. A roguish slap will be counter-productive. However, there is a solution. Simply get up and leave the room. Your partner will be left on his/her own feeling slightly foolish. Making your partner feel foolish is one of the chief weapons in the Improver's armoury.

13.

YOUR PARTNER NOISILY USES THE LAVATORY AT NIGHT, WAKING YOU UP

The solution here is neither the plumbing nor your partner's behaviour while in the lavatory, but your sleeping arrangements. Even if your partner were stealthily to use an open-necked bottle of Paul Masson Rouge while still in bed, it would probably still wake you up.

I like to take a tip from the redoubtable Marie Stopes, perhaps the single most influential British woman of the twentieth century. She maintained that husbands and wives (her 1918 bestseller *Married Love* was emphatically ***Married*** *Love*) should have separate sleeping accommodations. I can do no better than quote her directly:

> In the rather trivial terms of our sordid modern life, it works out in many marriages somewhat as follows: the married pair share a bedroom, and so it comes about that the two are together not only at the times

of delight and interest in each other, but during most of the unlovely and even ridiculous proceedings of the toilet. Now it may enchant a man once perhaps even twice or at long intervals to watch his goddess screw her hair up into a tight and unbecoming knot and soap her ears. But it is inherently too unlovely a proceeding to retain indefinite enchantment. [...] Whenever the finances allow, the husband and wife should have separate bedrooms. No soul can grow to its full stature without spells of solitude. A married woman's body and soul should be essentially her own, and that can only be so if she has an inviolable retreat.

Hear, hear.

14.

YOUR PARTNER EARNS MORE THAN YOU DO BUT NEVER PAYS FOR ANYTHING

Firstly, at what stage are you in your relationship? Secondly, do you have a joint bank account? Thirdly, are you a man or a woman? No adequate solution can be attempted until these questions are answered in full.

Financial asymmetry – which fluctuates from year to year, month to month, or minute to minute – is one of the most important dynamics of any partnership. It should never be blithely assumed, even in the modern era, that couples should maintain rigorous parity in financial matters. This would be dull. Who owes what to whom is sometimes the only thing that keeps couples together. Money is, in the broadest sense of the word, a currency.

Consider the following: a young couple, David and Christina, not yet married, engaged, or even particularly fond of each other, have contracted the habit of visiting exhibitions together. David earns a good deal more than Christina, having a senior position in a company exporting rococo mouldings to the Far East, while Christina runs a small but highly-thought-of charity for autistic pets, much patronized by various celebrities (which is the only reason he is with her in the first place, he being strikingly handsome, and she being the sort of girl who substitutes fizz for personal charm). For him to pay for her would be easy, but for her it would destroy any control she has over the relationship. It is essential for Christina that she stump up for those expensive return tickets to London, as well as the exhibition and the meal and show afterwards. There is nothing David can do but protest feebly, noting the adamantine glitter of her eyes as she pulls out her purse for the umpteenth time that day.

For male readers of this book who are wondering where they can find a partner like Christina, I would suggest that Christinas probably come to you with differential frequency if you are, like David, a) rich and b) strikingly handsome.

15.

YOUR PARTNER COMES INTO THE ROOM WHILE YOU ARE WATCHING TELEVISION AND SAYS 'YOU'RE NOT WATCHING THAT RUBBISH AGAIN, ARE YOU?'

One possible approach to this is to switch the television off, even if it is at a climactic point in *Crime Scene Investigation* or *The Only Way is Essex*: your partner will not be expecting you to do this, thinking they have the easy advantage of your divided attention. But Partner Management is more important than any transient entertainment. Then turn to your partner and say: 'I've been meaning to speak to you for some time about this, but my tastes in anything – television, art, books, music – are not inferior to yours, merely different. I would appreciate being able to watch what I wish to watch without interruption.'

Unfortunately this will then lead into a long debate about exactly whether it is *objectively true* that your tastes are merely different rather than being inferior; but you will unfailingly win the argument, even if you objectively do have lower tastes. The reasons are threefold:

a)   Your partner almost certainly wants to watch something else, which is the reason they made the comment in the first place. The debate is fruitlessly taking up their time, as it is yours: if you can go longer than they can, you will emerge the victor.

b)   The longer you leave the television off, the more you are demonstrating that you are *not* in thrall to whatever rubbish you happened to be watching.

c)   When the argument ends, you will still be in possession of the best chair, and clutching the remote control.

You may have to repeat the procedure once every three months or so, but the above is absolutely cast-iron.

16.

YOUR PARTNER TELLS THE SAME JOKES OVER AND OVER AGAIN

None of us is perfect in this area, I fear: if forced to produce a joke, I always tell exactly the same one, which involves standing still, moving one arm up and down in a flapping motion, and asking 'What's this?' The answer, 'a seagull coming back from the library', usually elicits puzzlement rather than laughter (the seagull has to carry her books under one wing). But *I* find it funny, which I suppose is why I go on telling it.

What to do, though, if your partner, similarly unblessed with a sense of humour, insists on actively volunteering the same jokes again and again?

Ways to crush your partner's performing spirit immediately suggest themselves: you could, for example, buy tickets in the front row of a comedy club and arrange for your partner to be comprehensively humiliated by a stand-up comedian. But you probably don't want a partner who is crushed; it has unfortunate impacts on other areas of life. What your partner needs is an awareness of the effect their behaviour is having on you (which is the important thing). Before going out for the evening, try actually requesting a particular joke. When your partner says: 'Oh, you mean the one about the…' say 'No, no, no, no, no, no, *nooo*, not that one.' 'Then you mean the one about the…?' 'No, no, no, no,' you say. 'I remember you telling that one at my brother's wedding. And again at the speech you made at the Hunt Ball. No, it was another one. A funny one.' Work your way through your partner's repertoire in this way. At the end of it, say: 'Well, I can't remember which one it was. Certainly not any of the ones you mentioned.' Your partner will then have a good idea of how familiar you are with their material, if nothing else, and will think twice before producing any of these jokes in your presence.

17.

YOUR PARTNER IS A PETTY THIEF

By this I mean specifically that your partner habitually removes things from other people's houses without permission: items of silverware, small *objets d'art*, books, etc. It is not done with any particular desire for profit, but out of a magpie-like attraction to shiny or valuable objects, or possibly a love of the thrill of transgression. Unfortunately this habit can lead to unpleasantness, or even legal proceedings.

Your partner obviously needs professional help, but in the meantime, the objects need to be returned discreetly to their owners. How to accomplish this? Simply post any item back with a note: 'I am a career criminal. Several nights ago I broke into your house and removed this article. Since then I have converted to Buddhism and realised the error of my ways. I beg you to accept it back.' Your host will realise that this story is nonsense but will be unable to decide which of his recent guests was responsible, and will feel that, instead of a serious attempt at burglary, he has merely been the target of a good-natured practical joke.

If your host has a housekeeper, the object can simply be posted to their care without any note.

18.

YOUR PARTNER FAILS TO TRIM THEIR NOSE HAIR

Nose hair is an odd phenomenon: it often seems that it can only be seen by its possessor in certain lights, or in profile, so that they may not be aware that they have tendrils protruding so far from their nose that the hair is actually curling and penetrating the opposite nostril.

Be ready to exploit opportunities such as the following: a group of people are seen laughing together at a social gathering. Your partner wonders what they are laughing about. Say: 'Actually, I know the cause. I walked past just now on the way to the buffet table. They're being rather cruel about Roger. It's his nasal hair. He's got so much of it that it's sometimes mistaken for a Hitler moustache. It seems to afflict men of a certain age. You can't see it in the mirror, you see.'

If your partner is a woman, substitute 'Roger' with 'Tamsin', and 'men' with 'women'.

19.

YOUR PARTNER REFUSES TO BREAK OFF A FRIENDSHIP WITH A FORMER LOVER

At parties, the former boyfriend or girlfriend is there, in the same room, talking to your partner, sharing a joke; the two are really hitting if off and laughing uproariously. Everyone present is thinking: 'These two still really get on well together; I wonder what the other half thinks of that?' You catch a stray glance between your partner and their former lover: it is the glance of two people who can never quite forget that they once went to bed together. And if this goes on, the possibility is that they will do so again. It would only take a fumble for coats after a few drinks; a stray hand in the back seat of a taxi; or a stroll away from the main body of guests at a summer party and a surprise visit to a greenhouse – 'Now these are interesting... these plants survive exclusively on air; they need no soil or water at all.' 'I know how they feel. I've felt like one of these plants for the last three years.' 'Oh Sandy,' etc.

Now, adultery is not necessarily unsurvivable (see §82), but you may wish to forestall it before it can develop. Subtlety will not work here. Instead of maintaining a merely cool relationship with the former lover, insult them completely and publicly. Go up to them and say something such as: 'You know, I think your clothes are a bit whiffy', or 'You remind me of the late Pope. You know, after he died.' Now you and this person can never appear in the same room again. If your partner continues to see them privately, that is adultery, and can be treated as such.

20.

YOUR PARTNER IS FANTASTICALLY ABSORBED IN THEIR WORK

If your partner is making a great deal of money, it's probably best to let them get on with it. If you demand a 'relationship' as well as cash, you are fantastically self-absorbed.

If, on the other hand, your partner is struggling and the bills are going unpaid, and you are burning the furniture for warmth, then it's probably best to issue an ultimatum: find a job that pays, or it's goodbye.

It all really hinges on what a partner is for.

Reasons to enter a partnership include a) love, b) sex, c) money, d) mutual support amid the vicissitudes of life, e) housekeeping, f) children, g) intellectual stimulation, h) the sharing of hobbies, i) insurance against loneliness, j) nursing care, k) the boosting of egos, l) respectability, m) religious duty, n) the satisfaction of parents, o) the cementing of dynastic bonds, p) the paying-off of a mortgage, q) for spite, r) for the potential benefits of divorce, s) for protection,

t) to make someone else jealous, u) because one partner is famous, v) because both partners are famous, w) because your partner was a bargain, x) because your partner has a single extraordinary talent, y) because your partner shares your tastes in home furnishings, or z) because your partner always leaves the lavatory seat (i) up or (ii) down. Various combinations of these possibilities may apply.

If you bewail the absence of any one of these in the presence of a good number of the others, you are unrealistic.

21.

YOUR PARTNER DOES AN IMPRESSION OF A PAKISTANI

This is racist and must be met with zero tolerance.

You should consider measures to drag your partner into the 21st century. Bringing a Pakistani home for dinner and announcing to the assembled company: 'My partner does a very funny impression of a Pakistani', is probably too farcical a solution. You could however buy a DVD of *My Beautiful Launderette* or *Bend it Like Beckham* and give it to your partner as a present, enabling them to develop a more nuanced picture of the way people from the Subcontinent actually speak and behave.

If this fails, increase the cultural pressure. Introduce the music of Nusrat Fateh Ali Khan or the Sabri Brothers at social gatherings, or consider converting to Sufism.

If none of this works, retaliate by replying in a Welsh accent.

22.

YOUR PARTNER'S CHILDREN BY A PREVIOUS MARRIAGE ARE WILD BEASTS, AND WHEN THEY VISIT THEY TURN YOUR WELL-ORDERED HOUSE UPSIDE-DOWN

This seems at first like an intractable problem. Children, once allowed to develop into wild beasts, are very hard to turn. But the problem is simply countered. Every time they visit, make sure they are presented with the very latest in video and gaming entertainment. Computer and television screens act on children much as sugar-water does on laboratory rats; they will do anything for more. Naturally, you will be turning them into Epsilon Minus Semi-Morons, fit only to be lift-attendants in later life, but they're not your children, are they?

23.

YOUR PARTNER AVOIDS PAYING THE BILL WHEN DINING OUT WITH FRIENDS, GOING OUT TO THE LAVATORY AT EXACTLY THE RIGHT MOMENT

If you have a joint account, this sort of behaviour hardly matters; but if you are either unmarried or keep separate finances, it can be a major problem.

The remedy is to delay payment until your partner is back at the table. Unless your partner is in the habit of actually going into the car-park and waiting in the car, they will perforce at some point return. You need to reserve your most sparkling anecdotes for this point of the evening, distracting everyone for as long as it takes for your errant partner and their credit card to make a reappearance. Alternatively choose this moment to produce a book of Magic Eye paintings and challenge the assembled guests to help you 'see' the images. People will immediately flock to your side with advice, and you can reasonably delay 'seeing' anything at all until your partner gets back.

24.

YOUR PARTNER WANTS TO BE HAPPY

This may not seem a problem at first sight, but consider this: relations between people depend to a large extent on establishing a status quo, or equilibrium of forces. One couple I know describes their relationship as one in which each side preserves an 'armed neutrality'. The search for happiness is as potentially disruptive to this delicate state as an extra-marital affair. Happiness-seekers incline towards religious conversion, the purchase of expensive gym equipment, random acts of kindness, the enlarging of comfort zones, laughter therapy, learning to paint, pilgrimage to foreign parts, etc.

The happiness industry is enormously influential and powerful. It has the backing of the dominant forces in our culture: advertising, television, books, colour supplements and Hollywood movies. It is very hard to counter.

The only true counter-ploy, if your partner insists on searching for happiness, is to introduce them to the virtues of misery. Misery-chic is just as compelling, in its own way, as happiness-chic. Usually it is less expensive. Examples of misery-chic include any of the cultural products of Norway, the art of Kathe Kollwitz,[3] the tango, the novels of Yukio Mishima, and so on. In extreme cases you may wish to encourage your partner to become a Goth.

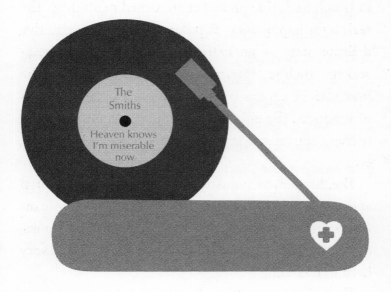

---

3 'The lithograph series 'Tod' (Death) from 1934/5 expresses the artist's 'deep sense of the futility of life and her longing to die'.

25.

YOUR PARTNER DOESN'T SUPPORT YOU IN ARGUMENTS WITH FRIENDS

How you respond to this probably depends on how you see your partnership in general. A healthy relationship is not necessarily one in which both parties wear matching knitted scarves and say everything in unison. Friends enjoy seeing a good-natured disagreement developing between couples, and regard unanimity as sign of weak-mindedness.

Next time, surprise your partner by amplifying and exacerbating the disagreement, taking it to a new level of combativeness. This will interest your friends and give your partner a taste of their own medicine.

26.

YOUR PARTNER IS BISEXUAL AND INSISTS ON A CONTINUED 'RIGHT OF EXPRESSION' IN THIS AREA

Your partner is very clever, having disguised the wolf of polygamy in the sheep's clothing of political correctness.

You probably wish to discourage this behaviour. However, you should reflect whether you wish to do so because a) you are jealous or b) because it brings social disgrace. If the latter, you are probably misguided. Your partner will gain social cachet by their fashionable antics, and you, as the tolerant bystander, will attract respect and perhaps sympathy. Your partner's behaviour will also signal to any of your own potential admirers that you may be available.

27.

YOUR PARTNER REFUSES TO EAT FOREIGN FOOD

In the privacy of your own home, your partner's unadventurous palate need not necessarily be of any concern. But if your partner rejects foreign cuisine offered at dinner parties, weddings, charity events, etc., they will look unsophisticated; and so will you, by association.

People rarely refuse to eat something merely because they dislike the taste of it. There are three main reasons why people turn up their nose at foreign fare: a) they are squeamish, b) they are snobbish, and c) they are hidebound.

These may be tackled separately.

If your partner is squeamish, for example about eating chicken feet, simply starve them before any important dinner. It is amazing what a true appetite can do to demolish food prejudice.

If they are snobbish, make great play with the fact that the Dalai Lama eats chicken feet, or that everyone in fashionable circles is now eating them (whether or not this is the case).

If they are simply hidebound in food matters – too conservative to try anything new – impress on them the fact that the food in question is not really foreign at all: point out that people have been eating chicken feet in Norfolk for years. This is usually safe, because there are very few things that haven't been eaten in Norfolk for years (including each other).

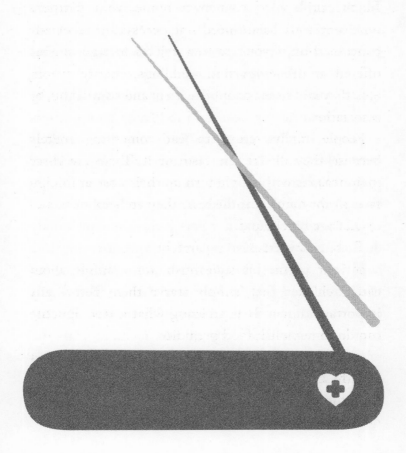

28.

YOUR PARTNER IS RUDE TO WAITERS

Many people like it when their partner is brusque with servitors. They think it shows masterfulness. If you are an Improver, however, it is likely that you find this sort of behaviour wanting in taste.

Let's take a situation in which a partner, smouldering with rage at having been told to 'Enjoy' by a waitress a quarter of their age, then finds that their duck is overcooked and dry. The partner calls the waitress over and points this out in no uncertain terms, loudly enough for the rest of the restaurant to hear.

Of course your partner gets a replacement bloody duck, but at what cost to you? You need to nip this behaviour in the bud. You can do so by means of the *Down and Out in Paris and London* Technique, otherwise known as the Orwell Manoeuvre. Present your partner with a copy of this memoir, with the relevant passages marked. These should make it very clear that any deviation from complete acquiescence and humility in the restaurant will lead to an absolute frenzy of revenge in the kitchen. The serving staff, you see, are not actually your friends. They are hoping for a tip. When they realize they are not going to get one, their feelings for anyone who humiliates them in public will approach outright hatred, and they are in the perfect position to retaliate.

Spitting in your food, in short, is the very least that they will do. I sometimes wonder how politicians ever have the nerve to dine out.

29.

YOUR PARTNER IS TIMID

I can highly recommend Toastmasters to build confidence. Toastmasters is nothing to do with making a really good slice of toast. It is a speaking club for people who wish to be able to perform in public or overcome shyness. The club holds meetings at hundreds of locations in the UK and worldwide. Members are encouraged to speak on subjects that interest them, and may also, as their experience grows, take part in 'table topics', in which they speak *ex tempore* on a subject that is presented to them in a sealed envelope. The experience is terrifying, but, as with childbirth, after it is over it is difficult to imagine being embarrassed about anything else ever again.

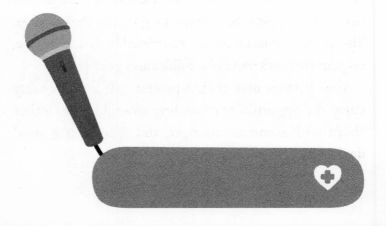

30.

YOUR PARTNER HAS NO DRESS SENSE

Your partner habitually wears clothes that are too young for them; they fail to wear clothing appropriate to occasions or the season; they wear the same clothes until they fall apart: these and many other problems fall into this general area.

It is very problematic to give anyone – even someone as close as a partner – that is, assuming you are close to your partner – advice on clothes. It is rather like giving someone advice on trimming their nose hair (see §18) or dribbling (see §44). One time-honoured solution is to get someone else, whose friendship is expendable, to do it for you. However, there is an easier way. Buy your partner a voucher for some new clothes, and hire a high-end personal shopping consultant to go with the voucher. This personal consultant can be briefed by you, of course, on your partner's particular foibles and grumps.

Your partner may at first protest, but will probably enjoy the opportunity of trailing around a few clothes shops with someone younger, and will learn a good deal from the experience.

31.

YOUR PARTNER VOTES FOR THE OTHER SIDE

A partnership in which two people have different political opinions can be a perfectly harmonious one. Politics is largely a matter of taste, analogous to taste in music. Political life in Britain, thank God, rarely requires that anyone actually *do* anything.

However, imagine a partnership in which one partner listened only to Tangerine Dream and the other only to the works of Delius. Or in which one half listened to music of the English baroque and the other to music of the French baroque. Frictions would almost certainly arise.

And what if your partner insists on voting for a party that is truly offensive, such as the BNP or the Greens?

I recommend a moral debating club. This is a club in which members thrash out their stance on issues of the moment. The purpose of such a club is not to come at any one issue from a party-political viewpoint, but for members to see where they stand morally on issues such as censorship, immigration or selective infanticide. Only after you have worked out your own ideas do you then need to choose a party that best represents these ideas. With a little guidance, your partner can very probably be made to see the error of their ways and weaned off whatever political party they have misguidedly identified themselves with. Your partner has probably been voting the way they do out of tribal loyalty or mere laziness.

32.

YOUR PARTNER CONTROLS YOUR SOCIAL LIFE

You have a partner who seeks to dominate you. He or she insists that you stay at home, and ridicules you if you attempt to go out or try new things – or forbids you outright to do them.

Frankly, I have no sympathy. You probably married or otherwise became attached to your partner precisely because of this propensity in them. You enjoy being dominated. Many people do. You probably also enjoy complaining to your friends about your partner's domineering ways, enabling you to bond with those friends (doubtless they are similarly oppressed, this being why you chose them in the first place). You enjoy having your freedom restricted. *Pace* Kierkegaard: 'Anxiety is the dizziness of freedom.' If you were allowed free rein you might not be successful in doing all the things that you think that you wish to do: roller-blading, travelling to foreign parts, forging exciting new friendships. Your partner's actions in restricting you are providing you with a valuable service. You enjoy the quarrels that you have with your partner over matters of personal freedom: these quarrels are the most intense episodes of a dull life. You also enjoy the making-up afterwards, with its associated kisses and presents.

Seek to improve your partner in this area and you will live to regret it.

33.

YOUR PARTNER IS A WINE SNOB

I know someone whose job it is to write the labels on wine bottles: she sits at home in her nightdress in front of the computer, without having seen, smelled or tasted the wine in question, and simply *makes it all up*. By a judicious manipulation of the terms 'well-rounded', 'smooth', 'medium-bodied', 'clean flavour', 'spicy finish', 'well-balanced', 'endearing intensity', and 'good with a stir-fry, pasta in cream sauce, light salads, gorgonzola, goat's cheese, venison, tomato-based pasta, grilled meats, pot roast, appetizers, pesto and all other foods and some minerals' she can generate a wine label for one of the major supermarkets in a few seconds. It is apparently very poorly-paid work, because most people, with a brief period of training, can do it easily.

If you do not happen to have such a friend to introduce your wine-snob partner to, I recommend pointing them to the latest research that says that most people are unable, blindfolded, to tell the difference between red and white wine, let alone agree on whether it is 'endearingly intense' or merely 'intensely endearing'. Put your partner through such a test (never force a partner: let them suggest it themselves, if possible). For safety's sake, make the test slightly harder: ask them for example to distinguish between six named whites. They will almost certainly do very poorly.

Alternatively on the MUT/GOF[4] side, you may wish to develop your own brand of hyper-snobbery and talk boringly to friends about how varietal marketing has superseded *terroire* marketing or how vulcanism can affect Chilean wines, which must be strained to remove tufa. Actually strain it there at the table; if in a restaurant, ask for a sieve to be brought.

The enjoyment of wine is all well and good, but the well-bred rarely go beyond comments such as 'tasty' or 'yum yum', or, if nasty, 'that reminds me, I must clean the windows' or 'I think my uvula has caught fire'. People assume these remarks indicate more knowledge than the speaker wishes to let on.

---

4 Mirroring of Undesirable Traits/Go One Further.

34.

YOUR PARTNER LAUGHS IN AN IRRITATING WAY

Naturally you should never descend to outright criticism of a flaw such as this: a direct rebuke is the best way to ensure a partner does nothing about it, in a defiant 'it's my laugh and I have a perfect right to it' spirit. Nor should recordings of the laugh be covertly made and then played back at an opportune moment. There are no opportune moments to play back such recordings that do not immediately lead to counter-accusations of infringement of privacy.

The best way to tackle the problem is to develop an irritating laugh yourself. Try a single, ejaculatory 'Ha!', sufficient to raise your auditor a good three inches in their chair, or a wheezing 'Sis, sis, sis' between your teeth which goes on for much longer than any conceivable joke could have merited. Soon you will be attracting sharp looks. Eventually your partner will say something such as: 'That noise you are making is very strange. I can't say I've noticed it before.'

'Oh, I'm sorry,' you should say. 'Is it irritating? I wasn't aware I was doing it. I expect you get the same sort of comments from people at work, don't you?' 'No,' your partner will reply, puzzled. 'Why would they say anything to me?' 'Oh, you know,' you say, 'that little trick of yours, throwing back your head and whinnying like a foal. It doesn't bother me in the slightest, but I can imagine people who are not familiar with it finding it somewhat unusual.'

35.

YOUR PARTNER NEVER TOUCHES YOU IN PUBLIC

If your partner never touches you in public it's possible they never touch you in private either, in which case you may be living in a loveless marriage. This is entirely normal.

New age therapists would have you believe that it's possible to revivify sagging libidos by having baths together with scented candles or going on holiday together to romantic destinations such as the Taj Mahal. This is wrong. A scented bath together will only enable you to scrutinize in detail exactly what you no longer find appealing about one another, and a holiday wandering around a romantic ruin will leave you bored and irritable and suspicious that all the other couples there are having the same problems as you are, or are much happier than you are, which is worse. Better to do something together that develops your partnership in a new direction: go on holiday to the war-torn Congo Basin, for instance, where you will be forced to cling to one another physically for support.

Also bear in mind that other people like nothing less than seeing couples who are obviously in love/lust with one another: it makes them feel their own relationship is lacking in this department. If you have a partner who never touches you, he or she is behaving with proper consideration for the feelings of others.

36.

YOUR PARTNER IS A USAGEASTER

A poetaster is someone who thinks they can write poetry when they can't; a usageaster is someone who thinks they know all about English language usage when they don't. Typical statements of a usageaster are: 'You should never begin a sentence with a conjunction,' 'You should never end a sentence with a preposition' and 'the actual name of Lincoln is Shrewsbury'. Late-stage usageasters often go around with a marker pen correcting shop signs and council notices. What is at fault is chiefly a want of consideration for others: anyone who says or does such things is simply showing off.

How to stamp out such an offender? Half of what they say will be based on nothing more than ill-informed smugness. Don't point this out directly: buy or borrow a copy of *The Living Language of English* by R Foate. Leave it lying around and occasionally read passages out aloud, particularly the following, from Mr Foate's introduction: 'The corpus of English evolves over time, and what is correct in one era may be incorrect in another.' You may even wish to make up sentences as you read. Try something such as: 'Particularly insidious are those who insist on the correct placement of grammatical entities such as prepositions and conjunctions. These are often men and women of a certain age who fret about sexual immorality and standardized fruit lengths.'

37.

YOUR PARTNER IS OFFHAND WITH THE KOREAN GARDENER

If your partner continues to be rude to Mr Kim, who will do the gardening? Foreign servants must be extended every consideration. We were all immigrants once.

If your partner is offhand, dismissive or brusque, this probably stems from feelings of misplaced superiority. Your partner must be made to feel the gardener is his equal. Why not introduce your partner to a little Hangul? Hangul is the Korean writing script. It looks rather like a knitting diagram, and learning it produces the same effect in the brain as trying to do *The Times'* crossword while undergoing knee surgery. Anyone who can understand it is clearly a genius.

38.

YOUR PARTNER USES AIR-FRESHENING PRODUCTS

The use of air-fresheners is perhaps the most infallible sign of poor taste. Whether they be in the drawing-room, the bedroom or the lavatory, air-freshening sprays, 'wicks' or 'plugs' send this message to your guests: 'Your body odours are offensive and need to be covered up by a nasal-membrane-stripping chemical miasma from Tesco.' It's quite possible that their body odours *are* offensive, but no well-bred person would dream of pointing it out.

If your partner is particularly addicted to lavatorial air-fresheners, and refuses to give them up, encourage them to substitute something appropriately medicinal, such as Friar's Balsam. A capsule of this squeezed into the sink will suggest that the previous occupant of the lavatory merely had a head-cold.

39.

YOUR PARTNER'S CHRISTMAS GIFTS ARE DISAPPOINTING

We have all heard of the husband who gives his wife the *Sheffield Snooker Companion*, or the wife who presents her husband with a weekend aromatherapy break for two in Dorking. These are unsophisticated ploys and I assume that your partner is better trained than to try them.

What, though, if your partner's gifts are simply meagre, cheap and unimaginative?

A good solution is a forcing approach in which you give your partner a gift that is obviously a great deal more expensive and thoughtful than the one they have given you (or that you anticipate they will give you). Anything personalized or monogrammed is ideal: an edition of a novel signed by their favourite author; a personalized Monopoly board featuring all their favourite locations; a bottle of perfume collected personally from Paris and unavailable elsewhere.

Another approach is to mention lavish gifts given recently by friends to their partners: 'I see Lucy got her own mount this year for the elephant polo bash in Selangar,' you say. 'I really wonder how Maynard does it.' If the elephant was personally collected from Nepal, say so.

Alternatively you may wish to emphasize (subtly) how cheap and nasty your partner's gift is. If you are a woman, and your husband has given you a pair of earrings of nickel-silver with cheap stones, put them in pride of place on your earring-tree surrounded by a selection of expensive and beautiful earrings, and then, in your partner's presence, get friends to admire the ensemble. The friends will completely ignore the cheap earrings but will spend a long time cooing over the expensive ones. This should give your partner an idea where he is going wrong.

In short, Christmas is a time for good will and spiritual reflection, but must not be neglected as an opportunity to work on your partner's shortcomings.

40.

YOUR PARTNER IS CONVINCED THAT HOMEOPATHY WORKS

Belief in homeopathy can be linked to emotions laid down in childhood. People will often say things such as: 'I remember when I was about six years old, my brother was stung all over by wasps and swelled up to three times his normal size, but my mother administered a Rescue Remedy and he was perfectly fine within hours.' Or: 'I remember when the tailor from the village got his foot caught in a man-trap; the flesh was cut right through to the bone but my father sent him off with a warning and some arnica, and within weeks he was back at his machine.' Asking such people to give up believing in homeopathy is tantamount to asking them to jettison some of their most treasured memories. So, while the little white pills can be annoying, try to be tolerant.

If offered them yourself, say that you are experimenting with a different alternative therapy – Chakra Rehydration or Peruvian Cheek Implants, for example – and the two can't be mixed for fear of life-threatening side-effects.

41.

YOUR PARTNER IS THINKING OF BUYING AN AMERICAN MOTORCYCLE

If your partner is having a mid-life crisis and is intent on purchasing some sort of transportation to go along with it, why not encourage them to get something that you too can enjoy – and enjoy in comfort, not sitting behind with your legs akimbo? After all, the cost of a new Harley Davidson can rise to £15,000 or more for the sort of top-of-the-range model that crises of personal identity usually require. For this sort of money you could buy a vintage Rolls Royce, Jaguar or Humber. Something with an arm rest on the back seat.

Your partner is probably meditating this purchase as result of seeing *Easy Rider*, *The Wild One*, or similar offerings. You may wish to tell them that Marlon Brando repeatedly disparaged this latter film, claiming it was the worst he had ever made, or that Jack Nicholson's character in *Easy Rider* was inspired by the Nevadan child molester Alfred G. Sable, who is still in prison.

If your partner thinks of themselves as something of a rebel, don't fail to point out the other middle-aged people of your acquaintance who have purchased similar expensive toys. A true rebel will be appalled at the thought of conformity.

42.

YOUR PARTNER TELLS ENDLESS ANECDOTES ABOUT CHILDREN FROM A PREVIOUS MARRIAGE

In these circumstances, children should be neither seen nor heard. Retaliate by talking about some much more distant connection: your second cousin's son, for example. Match anecdote for anecdote. 'My cousin's boy could hail a taxi on his own by the age of four', 'My cousin's niece by marriage has been asked to appear in the closing ceremony of the Commonwealth Paralympics,' etc. If you don't have a relative with an amusing life, make one up.

43.

YOUR PARTNER WISHES TO GET TO KNOW THE NEIGHBOURS

Your partner wishes to foster a sense of community by having a coffee morning, having a street party, tidying up communal areas, going on a nature walk, organizing evening classes with the neighbours as instructors, having a barbecue, pooling car journeys, or any of a number of other schemes.

You, however, are aware that your neighbours are witless, untrustworthy, dull or semi-mad, and you don't wish to sit through a coffee morning or stand up for hours holding pieces of blackened meat to be reminded of the fact.

The solution is to make yourselves the least desirable of all your neighbours. This can be accomplished quickly, simply and stealthily. Put a flyer through all the doors in the street with the message: 'The Watsons at No 23 [give your name and address here] are the approved agents for replacement windows and doors in your local area. Please contact either Gill or Dave on 07956 787652 [give a false mobile number here] for a quotation.'

Any overtures your partner then makes will be ignored.

44.

YOUR PARTNER DRIBBLES

If your partner has a medical condition or has just undergone root canal work, this is forgivable. If your partner habitually dribbles at night, staining the pillowcases, this is less forgivable, but there is little you can do except purchase plastic pillow-case inners (available from suppliers of incontinence products). If your partner dribbles in public to gain attention, letting a filament of spit hang from their lips before sucking it back up as it threatens to snap, they are probably a teenage boy. They will grow out of it.

45.

YOUR PARTNER'S RELATIONSHIP STATUS ON FACEBOOK IS 'IT'S COMPLICATED'

The available options for Facebook users to describe their relationships are: Single, In a Relationship, Engaged, Married, It's Complicated, In an Open Relationship, In a Civil Union, Divorced, Widowed and Separated. These all have something of the nature of carnival masks. They disguise, they hint, they deceive, they entice, they flatter. Even 'single', arguably the simplest, is fraught with ambiguities. Has the Facebooker listed themselves as 'single' because their lover is not on Facebook and cannot see it? Does the Facebooker have a different sense of what a relationship means, and is actually having casual relations with a number of people but doesn't regard them as 'serious' enough to merit a status change? And of the options, 'It's Complicated' is perhaps the vaguest and most annoying. It suggests that the Facebooker prefers to present their amatory activity as a fascinating drama, rather than simply being honest about it. It implies the existence of a love quadrangle at the very least, one that has been bodied into existence by the irresistible allure of the Facebooker themselves. It suggests that the Facebooker is probably a Social Media Oversharer who habitually talks about themselves in the third person ('Geoffrey Sanders is enjoying a nice lie-down with a copy of *The Bumper Book of Lolcats*').

If your partner has changed their status in this way then you have every reason to expect the worst. 'We need to talk' might be the most appropriate thing to say, if you can bring yourself to.

46.

YOUR PARTNER ONLY EATS ONE THING

This is actually a recognised medical syndrome: food neophobia, or the fear of new foods. Your partner will only eat Cadbury's Chocolate Fingers or Cheese Doodles. If allowed to persist, this can lead to liver failure, moulting, etc.

One solution would be to introduce a small portion of a healthier food, such as broccoli, onto your partner's plate at mealtimes, and ask them to eat a bite of it for every ten chocolate fingers they consume. This technique is only really useful for the very old or very young though, and is unlikely to be of much use in an adult relationship where you may not have complete dietary control. You could possibly ask your partner to try a new food for one week as a reward for some service on your part: putting out the rubbish, making the beds, vaccuuming, washing up, cleaning the car, or any of the other thousand duties that it is usually their job to perform for you. By the time a week has elapsed they will quite probably have absorbed the new substance into their repertoire.

Another approach is to tackle the problem by investigating its psychological causes. Your partner may feel that 'new' foods could harm them in some way, for example because they contain unknown additives or radioactive particles. You can counter this by telling them that you have secretly been injecting their chocolate fingers with ecto-carotinoids for the past six months, out of concern for their health. It obviously hasn't killed them so far so they may as well give up the struggle.

47.

YOUR PARTNER IS A CRASHING BORE

My own partner often bores me rigid. This is quite normal. It is inhuman to expect any partner to keep up a constant flow of novelty and epigrams. After the honeymoon period, filled with sweet days and roses, partnerships tend to settle into stasis.

On a typical evening, my partner and I sit at opposite alcoves of the drawing room, sometimes drawing, but more often reading. I might be dipping into *Marie Stopes' Very Large Handbook of Marriage* while my partner might be perusing *He Came on a Horse and 50 Other Unfortunate Book Titles*. We may not exchange a word the whole evening. Both of us find it a very satisfactory arrangement.

48.

YOUR PARTNER IS OBSESSED WITH WASHING DISHES BY HAND TO SAVE THE PLANET

The assumption of environmental obsessives and eco-bores everywhere is that the more laborious, inconvenient and old-fashioned something is, the better it must be for the 'planet'. This stems from a love of self-denial. Unnecessary privation is a powerful means by which to set one's life in order in an uncertain world. Washing dishes by hand and allied activities – cleaning rubbish before throwing it away, wrapping sandwiches in the plastic bags that the newspapers came in, opening toothpaste tubes with a scalpel to access the remaining paste – are means by which people seek to demonstrate their piety and abstemiousness in the face of widespread chaos and change. Some enclaves of Islington or Primrose Hill are more puritanical than 17th-century Nantucket.

Eco-beavers, I have noticed, also take a peculiar delight in handling their own waste. There may be some Freudian component to this.

However, the solution in this particular case is simple: it is a proven fact that a dishwasher, stacked full, uses far less electricity and water than heating water for hand-washing.

Don't expect your partner to receive this information with surprised delight.

49.

YOUR PARTNER IS ODD AROUND OTHER PEOPLE'S CHILDREN

I am presuming at this point that your partner is not a paedophile, registered or unregistered, and does not harbour inappropriate desires for the very young. Your partner's 'oddness' is probably attributable to their being unaccustomed to the presence of children, and thus unsure how to behave; they may also be worried that a natural affection for strange children may be mistaken for something more sinister, which leads them to behave oddly.

The remedy is to habituate your partner to children. You could try enrolling them as a lollipop person. Or you could encourage them to go along to primary schools as a volunteer to read stories to young children. Hard-pressed primary school teachers are often grateful for community volunteers in this area. Your partner will need to have a Criminal Records Bureau check, but this is usually a mere formality.

If they fail to pass this check, you will have found out something useful.

50.

YOUR PARTNER NEVER VARIES THEIR DANCE MOVES

James Brown said: 'I've got ants in my pants and I need to dance.' You could try this, but once the ants have been detected, your partner is likely to wish to leave the dance floor and visit the lavatory to get rid of them.

One tactic is to take the floor with your partner and then, just as they are getting into their routine, unchanged for the last twenty years, say: 'Hold this, would you?' Then give them your wallet, purse or glass, or, if at a dinner dance, an oversize pepper-grinder. They will be forced to integrate this unexpected item into their dance routine, eliminating some of its more offensive familiarity; they may even, zen-like, use the impediment to generate an entirely new repertoire.

51.

YOUR PARTNER MANGLES ENGLISH IDIOMS

Your partner does not speak English as a first language, and is often heard saying things such as: all bite and no bark, kick out a stink, I haven't got a faint idea, knee-height to a grasshopper, wheels within the wheel, an acid trial, add flames to the fire, all thumbs and fingers, hide into nothing, all over for the shouting, Dick, Tom and Harry, tight to the apron strings, at the top of my lung, just an average Joan, I don't have any hags to grind, have your work cut up, prove the pudding is in the eating, slow to the mark, how long is a string, the tail is whacking the dog, wake up for the coffee, every cloud has silver lighting, gone today gone tomorrow, part for the course, highway burglary, make a grade, scrapping the barrel, take it to a notch, shape up or ship up, be left holding the bag, plain as his nose on his face, pleased as sponge, pop a question, hair off the dog, take it on the shin, have a trick in his sleeve, look before you leak, a leg and an arm, rub salt in the womb, and so on.

If these locutions and others annoy you, the golden rule is never to correct your partner in public. This looks petty in the extreme. In private, I would suggest that there is only so much you can do, beyond using the idioms correctly yourself to set a good example. Frankly, my advice would be to rejoice in the colour these unorthodox usages bring your conversations. Your partner's versions are freshly minted neo-idioms, and should be cherished.

If you are unconvinced by this, try speaking their language.

52.

YOUR PARTNER READS IN THE LAVATORY

To keep a row of books in the lavatory is an extremely unhygenic practice. It is difficult to see how anyone could knowingly encourage a procession of people, all with unclean hands, to peruse such a collection. There is even a category of books known as 'toilet books', written and published for reading in the lavatory, sometimes by otherwise respectable publishers. If anything represents the nadir of literary effort and culture this must surely be it: the toilet book, a book requiring no commitment, which can be taken up or put down with equal indifference, soilable, disposable, flushable.

Added to the matter of hygiene, there is the fact that partners, if not actively discouraged, can begin to see the lavatory as a sort of second home. If you let your partner read in there, what will they start doing next? Writing postcards? Making phone calls? Eating lunch? Soon they will be spending hours in there when they could be doing something more worthwhile.

The first thing to do is to remove the lock on the lavatory door. Any door with a lock is always dangerous for the Improver. This now means that your partner can never be sure that they will not be interrupted, robbing them of some of the conventual peace of the smallest room. Pretend that the lock came off in your hand or needs to be fixed, but fail to fix it: your partner will find it difficult to protest, since there is no adequate explanation why they should care about it.

Secondly, remove the toilet library. Your partner will complain (feebly) but you should present it as essentially a cleaning problem. Books, after all, trap moisture, leading to mould on surfaces. Do not expressly forbid reading, but place the 'library' in a room at some distance from the lavatory, so that partners have to visit this other room to find an appropriate trivia-book. In half of all cases, this small extra effort will be sufficient deterrent. Subsequently remove the 'library' to an even further room, and then possibly to an outside shed. The toilet books can all then be accidentally burned on Guy Fawkes' Night.

53.

YOUR PARTNER REFUSES TO HELP WITH HOUSEHOLD CHORES

Naturally, a certain level of cleanliness should be maintained in the home, but *which* level? It is unlikely that any two people will share exactly the same tolerance for dirt and mess. What *you* perceive as your partner failing to help, out of laziness or slobbishness, might be perceived by them as a reasonable refusal to do something unnecessary, such as waxing the inside of the garage door.

Nevertheless, in a successful partnership, equilibrium must be reached, and it is desirable that you bring your partner up or down to your level of cleanliness rather than them bringing you up or down to theirs.

Let us say, then, that you are convinced that the inside of the garage door does need a wax, and wish for your partner to partake equally of the load. Begin by making a big fuss of this job. Do it with obsessive thoroughness, much more often than is necessary, taking a very long time about it, and *at a time which is inconvenient to your partner*, such as just before dinner or before giving them a lift to the station. Your partner will be forced to help, simply to get the thing done, and once inducted into the chore, can be more easily persuaded to do it in future. Other household tasks may be approached in a similar way.

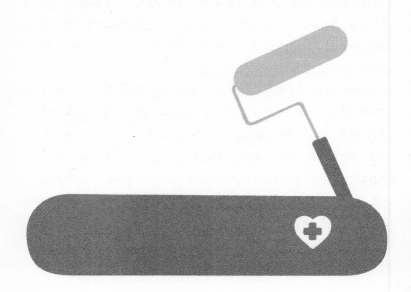

54.

YOUR PARTNER TALKS TO THE RADIO OR TELEVISION

This can be so maddening, after a decade or two, as to cause permanent scarring to the palms (caused by digging in of the nails to avoid crying out). After all, what could be more irritating than hearing your partner continually tell announcers: 'You must be joking!', 'What about China?' or 'Split infinitive!' However, it can be countered (and not by taking the obvious route of joining in with ironic comments of your own). Simply pretend to think your partner is going mad.

Approach them at first with a puzzled smile. 'You know that the man can't hear you, don't you dear?' (Say this with no irony whatsoever.) Then at a later date, refer to recent medical research: 'Naturally I don't mind if you talk to the radio, that's your business, but I was rather worried to see that it's a behaviour linked with Type 3 Proneural Abysmia. It might be worth a check-up, just to put your mind at rest.' Your partner will counter that their mind is perfectly at rest, thank you. Receive the information with relief. But then the next time, suggest that a tiny check-up might put your mind at rest. Finally your partner will see that the pleasure they derive from talking back to sports commentators and weathermen is offset by their irritation at being treated as though they might be mentally deficient.

55.

YOUR PARTNER FEARS THAT THEY ARE GOING MAD

This is not necessarily a bad thing (see above).

56.

YOUR PARTNER LOOKS LINGERINGLY AT THE LITHUANIAN CLEANER

Your partner is in love with the cleaner. Never mind that the two of you have been together twenty years and have raised three or more children, and that you personally have simultaneously pursued a career in international finance (if you have). Your partner is in thrall to someone who can barely speak English and is licensed only to handle bleach.

What to do? It's the human condition. Men lust; women lust. You are probably at fault for having agreed to engage a cleaner with attributes that appeal to the superficial aspects of your partner's personality.

The best solution is probably the following. Say to your partner: 'I see you are attracted to the cleaner. All right then, I give you full permission to have an affair with her/him. Let's see how far this thing goes. Be as unclean with the cleaner as you like. You may even make love in the house, as long as I am not also present. If, after a period of one month, you have managed to cement a real relationship with the cleaner, financially, spiritually and physically, then I will agree to a divorce on equitable terms. But if you have not, then the cleaner is to be sacked and replaced with someone more suitable. Until you are willing to accept this arrangement I must insist that you stop directing at the cleaner those distressing simpers.'

Of course, you do not need to be ready to condone an affair, but the foregoing speech should bring your partner down to earth.

57.

YOUR PARTNER LAUGHS WILDLY AT MANY THINGS BUT NEVER AT YOUR JOKES

Your partner has heard everything you have to say and is thoroughly bored by you. As mentioned above (§47), this is not necessarily a bad thing. There is no reason why you should interest your partner. That is not what partners are for. And their wild laughter in other contexts might not be true laughter but social laughter, designed rightly for the benefit of others. Your partner feels close enough to you not to bother laughing wildly at what you say. Mad laughter constantly ringing around the house would be something of a distraction, surely; almost grounds for divorce.

In summary, it is not necessary that your partner find you interesting, but it is necessary that they both be interesting to others and pretend to find others interesting, in order to reflect well on you.

58.

YOUR PARTNER'S MUSIC PRACTICE UPSETS THE NEIGHBOURS

I have a friend who plays the piano and lives alone in a six-storey terraced house in Edinburgh's New Town. Beethoven is her life. Recently the neighbours, who could hear her playing the piano at all hours of the day and night, complained. My friend politely declined to curb her practice hours, but did say (generously in my view) that she would be willing to bear a proportion of the costs for the neighbours to install soundproofed

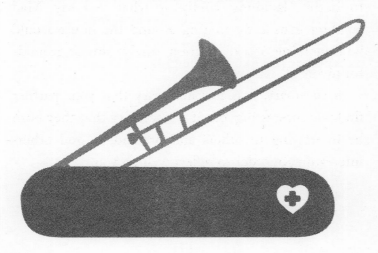

cladding in the walls of the room abutting her first-floor practice room. This the neighbours agreed to, with my friend bearing some 25% of the costs, which in total amounted to several thousand pounds. The cladding worked very well, but a few months after its installation, my friend fell out with her neighbours over the disposition of some hideous new wheelie bins introduced by the City Council. The dispute became so acrimonious that my friend decided to move her piano from the first to the second floor, negating the effects of the cladding. The neighbours responded by fitting more cladding on the walls of the second-floor rooms, this time without any financial contribution from my friend. My friend waited a matter of a week or so, and then moved the piano to the third floor. The neighbours responded again, and my friend moved the piano again. This game of cat and mouse continued until the neighbours' marriage broke down.

In short, whether this is a problem entirely depends on whether you like your neighbours or not.

59.

YOUR PARTNER'S FLAT IS SUFFUSED WITH A SWEETISH ROTTING SMELL

If your partner has recently had an acrimonious break-up with a previous lover, the curtain poles may be full of prawns. This is now a standard tactic for revenging ex-partners. It is highly effective because it is impossible to tell where the smell is coming from, and victims can be driven to ripping out floors and walls to locate the source of the offence.

Other popular gambits for revenging lovers (the Toothbrush Tamper Manoeuvre, the Single Lapel Cut-off, the Delayed-Action Weedkiller Lawn Expletive, etc) can be found in my forthcoming handbook *102 Ways to Revenge Yourself on Your Partner.*

60.

YOUR PARTNER BELCHES UNAPOLOGETICALLY AFTER MEALS

Murphy-Hurley in *Transactional Analysis for Dummies* notes that a strange reciprocal phenomenon exists: in cultures where belching after meals is looked upon favourably, or even regarded as good manners, it is not considered polite to ask a man after the health of his wife; conversely, in cultures where asking after the womenfolk is permitted or encouraged, belching is looked upon with disfavour.

Whether or not this is true, it can be used as a ploy in situations in which you wish to cure your partner of this habit. First, inform your partner of this little-known cultural phenomenon, and then, in a spirit of Retaliatory Echoing, simply ask 'How's your wife?' after every incident of belching, hoping that this becomes so irritating that your partner will eventually desist. This can obviously be done regardless of whether your partner is a man or a woman: it will be irritating in either case.

However, if your partner is impervious to this kind of suggestion, something more extreme may be required. The next time you attend a dinner party, look expectantly toward your partner and say to the assembled guests: 'Any time now Geoffrey/Laura will let fly with an absolute corker. Watch for it, everyone. It's really terrifically entertaining.'

If Geoffrey/Laura does then let fly with an absolute corker, you are sunk, unless you join in merrily with the applause.

61.

YOUR PARTNER NEVER MOVES FROM THE TELEVISION

If this is literally true, i.e. your partner is not employed and sits staring at the television from morn till night, you have a serious problem. Among other things, your partner is probably clinically obese. A completely sedentary existence spent being bombarded by advertisements for fast food, alcohol and other TV programmes will almost inevitably lead to catastrophic weight gain.

The solution to the problem is to 'go green'. Under the mantle of this fashionable ideology, almost any behaviour is permissible. For example, you could demand that your partner join you in an energy-saving drive, necessitating that the television only be switched on between certain hours. Even more drastically, you could hook your partner up to the television via some form of exercise equipment, such as a stationary bicycle. This would simultaneously control their weight and generate electricity for the home. If your partner is only allowed to watch those programmes for which they can generate the electricity, their viewing-time will almost certainly go down.

62.

YOUR PARTNER APPEARS TO BE EXAMINING YOU FROM OUT OF THE CORNER OF THEIR EYES

This is extremely unnerving, like being in a Hammer House of Horror film.

What to do? Keeping a battery of small cushions to throw is a possible counter-tactic. Examining your partner back out of the corner of your own eyes can also sometimes be essayed.

The most likely explanation for your partner's behaviour though is that they are wearing reading-glasses. If you are sitting to the side of them, your partner can only see you by a) turning their head and looking over the top of the glasses at you or b) glancing to the side past the frame; the second is less effort.

In short, your partner is probably not considering murdering you, and just wants help with the crossword.

63.

YOUR PARTNER INSISTS ON DYEING THEIR HAIR DESPITE THE FACT THAT IT LOOKS RIDICULOUS

To keep a head of hair dyed is a major undertaking. Your partner will have to commit themselves to spending thousands of pounds at the hairdressers just to keep the roots under control. Needless to say this could be better spent on things that are important to you.

Phase one is to convince your partner that they can't continue dyeing their hair forever. Sooner or later they will have to submit gracefully to the inevitable. Show them pictures of men and women who look good with grey hair: Susan Sontag, Helen Mirren, Simon Rattle, George Clooney. Then show them people who look ridiculous with dyed hair: no names need be mentioned here, but their ranks are legion. Then point out that prolonged use of hair dye is linked to extreme allergic reactions, psoriasis and other skin complaints. Tell them the story of Sacha Baron-Cohen, who was hospitalized after dyeing his hair for the film *Bruno*.

Then give your partner a projected hairdressing and medical bill for the rest of their life.

Phase two, once they have submitted to your logic, is to provide them with a method of becoming grey without having to go through the intermediate stage of 'growing out', so that it doesn't appear that a cup of milk has been poured over the crown of their head. Instruct their hairdresser to dye the hair in progressively lighter shades of grey-brown ('a darker shade of mouse') until the right tone for the natural head of hair is achieved.

64.

YOUR PARTNER IS UNLOVELY

Few of us are lovely. Of those who are lovely, the loveliness will fade. Develop the habit of seeing your fellow human beings as the seventeenth-century playwright John Webster did: beauty, for Webster, was only skull deep.

Of course, it is possible to improve a partner's unloveliness: that's what this book is about, after all. If your partner dyes their hair unnecessarily, belches unapologetically, laughs annoyingly or has protruding nose-hair, then please see the relevant section. But if, after every improvement is made, they are still unlovely, then you have come face to face with the human condition. To quote the King of Brobdingnag in *Gulliver's Travels*:

'I cannot but conclude the Bulk of your Natives to be the most pernicious Race of little odious Vermin that Nature ever suffered to crawl upon the Surface of the Earth.'

65.

YOUR PARTNER IS TOO LOVELY

This is the opposite problem. Your partner is too handsome (if a man) or beautiful (if a woman) or handsome (if a woman in a Jane Austen novel) for their, or your own good, and it helps you not a whit to remind yourself at intervals that your partner is a member of the aforementioned 'pernicious Race of little odious Vermin'. You catch other people looking at them admiringly. You wonder whether you can trust your friends not to try something. You dread the moment when you will be forced to fight for your right to keep them. You wonder how long it will be before they notice that they are too good for you.

Short of disfiguring your partner or forcing them to wear a niqab, your only option is to become beautiful yourself. That way you will achieve parity and your anxieties will slip away.

Of course, you cannot literally become beautiful if you are not beautiful. Personal grooming and surgery can only do so much in the face of age, sagging, etc. The secret is to *act* beautiful. Be terrifyingly self-possessed in the face of the people who guard VIP lounges. Also be very beaming and expansive with small children and animals, as if filled with relief because they are the only creatures on earth who will not take this as an immediate invitation to seduce you. Give the impression of being extremely clever (as all truly beautiful people do, through Tolstoy's Illusion[5]), regardless of whether you are or not; although you should disdain to offer any actual information on any topic, since this would be beneath you. All these gambits are well within the purview of anyone, no matter how personally attractive.

---

5 'It is amazing how complete the delusion that beauty is goodness.'

66.

YOUR PARTNER IS ALWAYS LATE

Take the case of Eugenia and Scott. Eugenia is a PhD student who teaches Spanish and Italian. Scott is a software designer who works at home and rarely gets up before noon. It might be expected that Scott would be the one who would always be late. In fact the problem lies with Eugenia. Scott waits around for her for hours, in cafés, bars at or his flat, getting increasingly angry.

The difficulty in this case is one of culture. Eugenia hails from a Latin culture in which it is acceptable to turn up for personal assignations one, two, even three hours late, with nary an apology. Scott, late-rising and vaguely fungoid as he is, comes from a Nordic culture where courtesy is parcelled out in minutes.

There is also a problem with Eugenia's sense of the value of Scott's time. Eugenia is aware that Scott has little else to do except tap on his keyboard, and thinks that it won't harm him to do a little more tapping while she talks to a friend or does some shopping between lessons.

The solution for Scott is to tell Eugenia to treat him much as she does her Spanish and Italian clients. She is never late for lessons, is she? Of course not. Henceforward, more than ten minutes late for a meeting with him and he will regard her as in breach of contract. He will certainly no longer be at the venue arranged. Eugenia should see Scott as a business client.

Scott needs to regain Eugenia's respect. The Mediterranean way of life is just a smokescreen in any case. Lateness is always a discourtesy: the reality is simply that in Mediterranean cultures people enjoy being rude to one another.

67.

YOUR PARTNER GETS CAR-SICK

The reason they get car-sick is because they are not driving. Put them in the driving seat and it will cure them.

The reason behind this, I am told, is that car-sickness occurs when the body is unable to predict which way it will be asked to move next. If the sick-prone person is able to control the movement (by being in charge of it), the body is allowed a small grace period to ready itself for the next turn, acceleration, deceleration, etc.

So: your partner is sick because they lack control. This has an obvious metaphorical significance in the sphere of your joint relations. Your partner is being made nauseous by *your* propensity to control things.

If this is the case, then this calls for some lateral thinking. On the principle that it is not motion that they are responding adversely to, but lack of control, give them a small amount of control in *another* area and the car-sickness problem will disappear. Let them choose the sandwiches for a long car-journey, for example.

68.

YOUR PARTNER HOGS THE DUVET

This mild-seeming problem can actually threaten partnerships. A recent survey put poor 'bediquette' as a cause of 18% of all break-ups, with 80% of people having at one time left the shared bedroom to sleep in another room.

However, there is a simple solution. Keep the double bed, but buy two separate single duvets. This is a solution favoured in Europe, where the duvet was common long before Britons developed a taste for it, and where a certain practical wisdom prevails. The two-single-duvet approach allows each partner to position the cover to his or her taste (duvet over head, at waist, etc.) and to choose an appropriate tog value, obviating quarrels over temperature. A very fat partner will always be cold under a duvet designed for a very thin companion, for example.

Another solution is to buy a king-size duvet for a queen-size double bed, and then tuck the duvet in smartly on *your* side.

Other bediquette matters involve grinding of teeth, sleep-talking, snoring, etc. This plethora of obstacles to a good night's sleep highlights the benefits of sleeping entirely separately, not just under separate duvets but under separate ceilings (see §13).

69.

YOUR PARTNER WISHES TO LIVE OFF THE LAND

There seems to be an increasing fashion for 'sustainability', 'going off the grid', 'self-sufficiency' and so on, as if we were not living, after all, in a society, but existed as autonomous, unconnected islands remote from the civilizing influences of culture, commerce, art, science and so on. Surrounding oneself with chickens and goats, shivering in the dark around a candle at night, and having one's clothing permanently impregnated with farmyard odours (wind turbines or solar panels generally do not allow luxuries such as a washing machine), seem to me entirely retrograde. For some it may conjure up visions of the 'good life': for myself it recalls the figure of Lennie in *Of Mice and Men*, who was fixated on getting a farm and keeping rabbits, and was finally driven to snap a girl's neck.

If your partner wishes to live off the land, the cure is to make them live off the land. Send them on an unaccompanied holiday via the organization Working Weekends on Organic Farms, which organizes stints of varying lengths – from a weekend to several months – doing backbreaking farm-work, laying plastic, humping pig-arks, etc. Book the holiday for some point in November. Your partner will end up in a damp caravan with no electricity, covered in manure, and within hours will be begging for release.

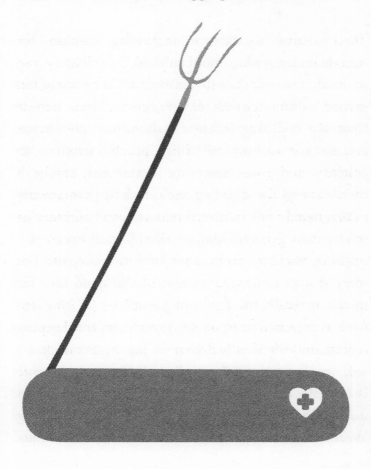

70.

YOUR PARTNER IS AN AGGRESSIVE DRUNK

Your partner's behaviour while drunk is not a problem of nature, but a problem of culture.

Studies have shown that different nationalities become drunk in different ways. The Finns become morose, the Argentineans salacious, the Persians poetic, and so on. The British become brutish. The recent attempt to create a more congenial 'café-style' culture with late night opening in British towns and cities merely led to the extension of breaking glass and screams from 12am to 3am. British people feel they are expected to become loud and obnoxious, so they do; if they were expected to become wry and philosophical, then they would do that.

The solution is to make friends in the Japanese community. It is a fact that in Japan, drunk people are even more friendly and polite than they are while sober (which is saying something). They spend their time filling up one another's glasses, laughing at one another's jokes, paying one another compliments, and exchanging business cards, which they arrange on their thighs with great care and formality even while they are simultaneously losing motor control.

Get your partner to drink with your new Japanese friends. Social conformity will do the rest.

71.

YOUR PARTNER WANTS YOU TO COME TO CHURCH WITH THEM

Your partner is religious and you are not, or (rather more seriously) your partner is of a different religion (or denomination) to you.

Your partner may wish you to come to church a) to convert you, b) for company, c) to meet their friends, d) to become closer to you spiritually, e) to stop you sleeping late on Sundays, f) to butter up the vicar, g) as a family outing, or h) other reasons. In fact there are as many reasons for going to church as there are people. Most of the reasons are not religious.

If, all things considered, you really don't wish to attend church, then you must find something else that demands your attention on Sunday mornings. If you subscribe to a different religion, you have a ready-made answer. If you have no religion, you can invent one. Some time ago I invented a religion called 'Sundayism', which was the world's first pay-as-you-go religion. Its adherents paid £50 to join, and with their application form were each allowed to invent an article of belief, to be submitted to the other members for approval. Thus dogma was built up by democratic accretion. It was, in its time, very successful, though schismatism has since taken its toll. Anyone interested in joining should contact me care of my publisher.

72.

YOUR PARTNER WEEPS WHEN THEY WANT SOMETHING

Even the greatest man can be brought low by a woman's tears. So runs conventional wisdom. There is no general consensus on whether the greatest woman can be brought low by a man's tears; one might suspect possibly not.

However, take the case of Maurice and Clarissa. Maurice weeps softly if Clarissa wishes to go out with her friends. Not loudly and demonstratively, you note, but softly and unobtrusively. In fact, Clarissa sometimes can't tell whether Maurice is crying at all. His expression does not alter; but, if she looks closely, there are the tears, singular and unwiped-away, resting cleverly half-way down each cheek. Clarissa is overwhelmed at these moments, and does not merely cancel her date but coddles Maurice for the rest of the evening.

Clarissa thinks that she has found a man who is in touch with his emotions, but in fact Maurice's behaviour will retain its charm only in the first six months of the partnership. After this Clarissa will begin to look at Maurice in a strange new way and wish for him to a) beat her at arm-wrestling, b) stop tidying away her things for her and c) stop having long intimate conversations with her mother.

The only way forward is to treat Maurice's tears with the contempt they deserve. There is only room for one man and one woman in any heterosexual partnership, and if the man starts becoming like a woman, the woman, out-womaned, may retaliate by becoming more like a man.[6] Clarissa must intrude forcefully on Maurice's own ground, and start weeping more often than he does, possibly while on the phone to *his* mother or otherwise aggressively multitasking (renewing the television licence; chopping carrots or treating other cylindrical objects roughly; etc).

---

6 Clarissa may have done this, and she may not; more information is required.

73.

YOUR PARTNER SENDS YOU SELF-DRAMATIZING POSTCARDS

Your partner has never quite got over the feeling, inculcated as an infant, that they are the centre of the universe, and behaves accordingly. They send you postcards with messages such as:

> Today I saw M. and we talked. I looked outside and saw a single violet trembling on the lawn. I threw myself to the floor, racked with sobs.

You must write back with postcards of your own, preferably seaside ones with blowsy captions, and on the back the words:

> Joey [or Henry, or Oscar] has got the runs and we have to keep him outside. Pizza and chips for dinner. Nothing on TV. The builders next door are making a hell of a racket. Keep your chin up!

74.

YOUR PARTNER UNDERSTANDS YOU

How bad could this be? Well, quite bad. Your partner appears to know all your thoughts. Even worse, they presume to know all your thoughts even if they don't. 'Here, you open the rollmops,' they say, handing you the jar and smiling dryly. 'I know you like the pop the lid makes.' This when neither of you has ever opened a jar of rollmops in one another's presence before. Have they confused you with a partner from a previous existence? More of this and it can get quite wearing. 'I bought you some of that calligraphy ink you like,' they say. 'It's from your usual shop.' Useless to protest that you have never attempted calligraphy and suffer from vibration white finger.

The solution is to invent fictional episodes in your own life that baffle your partner. Better still, make out that your life before you met was in every way more exciting, fulfilling and memorable, and more central to *the real you*. Into this throw a friend (fictional) whose job is to have shared these experiences and who knows you in a way that your partner could never do. 'Just got an email from Jake,' you should say. 'He still gets a Christmas card from the Home Secretary after that fracas when we were all unfairly banned from working for the civil service after the incident in the painter's cradle underneath the Clifton suspension bridge.' Your partner, unable to compete, will withdraw.

75.

YOUR PARTNER ALWAYS WANTS TO GO TO THE SAME HOLIDAY DESTINATION

Your partner always wishes at stay at 'The Old Horns', Clacton, Essex. Your partner is great chums with the landlady, enjoys the beach and the promenade, and talks to everyone, including the men who sell inflatable sharks. You are heartily sick of 'The Old Horns' and would rejoice if it burned to the ground, and the rest of Clacton along with it. What you would like is to rent a comfortable, well-equipped, centrally-heated two-storey house in Arapena, in the hills north of Rome, an ancient town steeped in history and art, where you could enjoy some walking and inspect the frescoes in the little hill churches.

On the face of it, an insoluble problem. But this year you have an important birthday coming up. Never mind that you are 35, or 43, or 61, or something equally undistinguished. This is 'the age daddy was when he died' or 'the last prime number year I feel I'll ever reach' or 'my last chance to get some real writing done before my xth birthday – and they say no one ever published a really great first novel after that year'.

Planning is the key. Start talking about the holiday well in advance, preferably when you're unpacking after getting back from Clacton. Harp on it regularly thereafter. Get photos and timetables for Arapena. Make the booking at least three months early, at a point where your partner feels vaguely that it will probably never happen.

Finally, make sure that it is a really good holiday, and that your partner really does love it and gets on well with the locals. Bribe the locals to be charming beforehand.

Your partner is a creature of habit: turn this susceptibility to your advantage by creating a new habit, this time an Italian one.

76.

YOUR PARTNER LOVES GIVING DINNER PARTIES BUT CAN'T COOK

A friend of mine was similarly afflicted. His wife was a great socialite but completely food-blind. He took to laying out snacks in the downstairs linen cupboard for people to fill up with; guests were secretly informed of the snack-cache and, as the evening progressed, went down one after the other, ostensibly for the lavatory, but actually to get something edible. It was a successful solution until the hostess discovered the cache and confronted her husband. 'Unreasonable behaviour' was I believe cited as grounds.

My friend had the right general idea but made the mistake of unnecessary subterfuge. It is always best to be open. The next time your partner decides to throw a dinner party, suggest that it might be fun to have a buffet party, perhaps in fancy dress. Allow your partner to do the cooking as usual, but then introduce a number of catered dishes onto the buffet table, 'to save you too much work while you get your costume ready'. Your partner, depending on how self-deluded they are, will welcome the competition, but will be able to see, after the party, which dishes have been touched and which haven't.

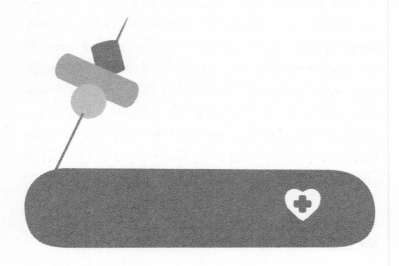

77.

YOUR PARTNER DOESN'T WISH YOU TO ACCOMPANY THEM WHEN THEY VISIT THEIR PARENTS

Do your partner's parents actually know about you? Is it possible that your partner is hoping to conceal you entirely? Were your partner's parents at the wedding or civil partnership? Cast your mind back. Or perhaps you are not married or civil-partnered, and just living together. Have your partner's parents ever visited? If so, were you referred to as 'my flat-mate', or something more substantial? If 'partner' was mentioned, was any space given to the idea that you might be a business partner? Did, on the occasion of the visit, your partner insist on showing them the spare room as if it were your bedroom?

Confrontation is key here. If your partner is not willing to advertise your partnership loudly and clearly for all to hear, you must demand that they do.

78.

YOUR PARTNER DRIVES UNDER THE INFLUENCE

In the past this was much more acceptable than it is now, to the point where partners would often claim to drive better when drunk, saying things such as: 'Unless I've had at least five gins I can't be trusted on the motorway.' Nowadays, in a climate in which it is expected that spouses will hide their partner's car-keys, or even turn their partner in to the police, much as children in *Nineteen Eighty-Four* would denounce their own parents, this attitude is socially unacceptable.

One solution is to give your partner a scare by doctoring the car so that the brakes fail and they leave the carriageway and drive through a hedge, narrowly missing a pregnant mother, but this is for Advanced Improvers only. A much more simple ploy is to tell everyone you know about your partner's propensity, letting them do the work of shaming your partner. This is the principle of Transfer of Disapproval. Utter no word of criticism yourself and instead cultivate an easy fatalism. Say to people (in your partner's hearing if possible): 'Of course I know that I'm going to end my days flung doll-like onto the verge like the last scene in *The Postman Always Rings Twice*. I've come to live with the idea. But I can't drive, and Geoffrey/Laura refuses to keep within the drink-driving limit. I just hope we don't take anyone else with us when the time comes.' The collective disapproval will be so potent that Geoffrey/Laura will be forced to become a teetotaller on the spot.

79.

YOUR PARTNER WON'T SHARE CHILDCARE

If the children in question are not your partner's children, then perhaps your partner has a point: she or he was not responsible for their arrival into the world, and has no genetic advantage to gain by their continued survival. But if the children are your partner's, and especially if they are solely your partner's and not yours, then you must assert your right not to be surrounded by unidentifiable slimy things and continual hitting, and must encourage your partner to play their part.

If your partner has a high-powered job that restricts their ability to share childcare, get a nanny, since you can probably afford it.

If your partner is merely lazy, don't be a martyr. Stop looking after the children. Stop making packed lunches for them, clearing up after them, reading them bedtime stories, etc. Go on strike, or feign illness. The children will demand these services from the next available pair of hands. Your partner will soon have a rich appreciation of the work you do.

If neither of you is willing to look after the children, have the children look after themselves. This is a much-neglected solution for children aged 3 and up. In large families of the past, care of the very young was delegated to the older children; there is no reason, if you have any older children available, that you cannot adopt this approach. Soon they will be doing all the work you used to do, and will grow up the more capable for it.

80.

YOUR PARTNER CRITICIZES THE WAY YOU DRESS

Don't take the approach of criticizing them back: this will lead to an increasingly frank exchange of insults. They will be accurate insults on your side, no doubt, but very hurtful ones on theirs. No, you should make your partner feel the stinging irrelevance and wrongness of this sort of criticism from a different direction. Brief an old-established friend or relative to sniff at your partner's fashion sense. 'Oh, not that hat,' they should say. Or: 'Those check trousers make me think of Rupert the Bear, I'm sorry.' The first time, because entirely uncharacteristic, this will be hurtful; the second time your partner will smell a rat.[7] 'Did x put you up to this?' they will ask, referring to you. Your friend or relative will reply ruefully (having been briefed to do so): 'Yes, all right, I admit it, but they asked me not to tell you. You see, x is so hurt by what you say to them that they thought you'd like a taste of your own medicine. You don't really have poor dress

---

7 I presume here your partner is of normal intelligence.

sense – I take back what I said about Rupert – but even though x sometimes dresses a little oddly, they do their best and they're terribly hurt if you don't like it. I think you'd do better just to put up with the clothes you don't like and remember that most of the time x gets it right.'

This should shut them up.

81.

YOUR PARTNER WANTS CHILDREN AND YOU DON'T

Take them to Alton Towers. On the long car journey there, talk to them about heritable diseases. As you are queuing for the Oblivion rollercoaster, tell them about the average cost of a child over a lifetime. Later, as they are picking the vomit from their hair, impress on them that children do not keep you young, but instantly propel you into old age.

82.

YOUR PARTNER IS CONDUCT-ING AN EXTRA-MARITAL AFFAIR

Let's take a couple, Evelyn and Richard, in their late forties. Evelyn has had numerous affairs, usually with married men, which Richard knew about at the time. Evelyn is tied to Richard through the children and the mortgage, and it would take much more than sexual novelty for her to leave him. Richard appreciates this and doesn't make a jealous scene, knowing it would be counter-productive.

In another scenario, Selwyn and Amanda, a couple in their early thirties, have been married for three years when Selwyn begins an affair with a girl in his seminar group at college. Amanda finds out, and physically attacks the girl, ripping her earring and removing a part of her ear. The police are called in and Amanda is arrested. Selwyn loses his post at the college and begins drinking, and Amanda, after her release from a three-month stint in prison caused by the fact that the girl is able to pay for a top-flight barrister, leaves Selwyn and gets a job as a social worker, which leads to her suicide. I mention this only because it happened to a couple I know (the names are changed).

In short, your approach to adultery will always be a matter of personal taste and choice, but if in doubt, I would recommend settling in for the long haul. It is a rule in these things that the wronged person usually comes out on top, in terms of the sympathies of others, the law, and their life prospects, whereas the adulterer, for all the immediate gratifications of love, will often wind up unhappy, stigmatized and out of pocket. Remember particularly that if you are married, the ace in your hand is a divorce settlement in your favour. Those who prefer to remain unmarried might wish to think about this.

83.

YOUR PARTNER ALWAYS LEAVES YOU ALONE AT PARTIES

Take a case study: Nadia, a woman of 31, is a failed novelist. She has produced three volumes in the last five years, all of which have gone straight to self-publication. Her husband, Castor, 25, is a successful pensions advisor. The relationship has been faltering in recent months due to Nadia's fear of abandonment in public places. Nadia fears that Castor, six years younger than she, might stray and find another woman, perhaps one who is able to attract a publisher.

At parties, Nadia has become extremely possessive, sticking Velcro-like to Castor and never letting him out of her sight. Castor attempts to get away, but Nadia has even been known to reorganize the seating arrangements at weddings so that she is able to be next to her husband.

The solution? Castor does not need improvement, Nadia does. Nadia is on course to wreck her marriage, and must realize this before it is too late. She would benefit from the following exercise. Next time Castor makes a bolt for it, Nadia should find the most attractive available man in the room and flirt with him. Castor will note this at first with amusement and relief, but this will soon turn to perplexity, and finally to jealousy. This will act as a tonic to the marriage. Nadia will get her self-confidence back and Castor will gain a new respect for her.

Alternatively Nadia should consult a psychiatrist.

84.

YOUR PARTNER NEVER LEAVES YOU ALONE AT PARTIES

If the above is the case, your name may be Castor and your partner's name may be Nadia. You may be a successful pensions advisor.

What to do if you are a Castor? You need to help your partner overcome her fears, simultaneously giving you back your own freedom of movement.

This can be accomplished via a simple ruse: at parties, arrange with a fellow guest that they buttonhole your partner and engage them in conversation. Of course, your partner might have few conversational resources, and so it might be difficult to find a guest willing to take on this task. As with anything in life, you must appeal to self-interest. Say: 'My wife [if it is a wife] is a little shy in social situations, and you would be doing me an enormous favour if you were to draw her out. As it happens she's very interested in medieval privies' (insert the object of the fellow-guest's area of expertise here) 'and I'm sure she'd be fascinated if you'd tell her about your latest research.' Thus two objectives can be accomplished at once: the flattery of a fellow guest and the decanting of your partner.

Dog-like devotion is attractive in a life-partner, but may attract social ridicule. Ensure your partner fits somewhere in the spectrum from dog to human being.

85.

YOUR PARTNER PEES ON THE FLOOR/SEAT/CURTAINS

The problem may well derive from carelessness rather than malicious intent. Try leaving a large pile of paper towels and some disinfectant in the lavatory. The problem may well be that your partner doesn't have the materials to clean up afterwards and is embarrassed about going to the kitchen to get them.

Alternatively, leave some towels on the floor where your partner tends to 'miss'. These prevent staining to the floor, facilitate cleaning up, and enable your partner to see immediately that they have failed to score a direct hit. With luck their behaviour will improve to the point where the towels are no longer necessary.

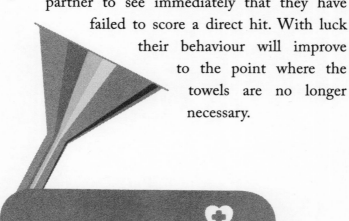

86.

YOUR PARTNER IS GAINING A SHOCKING AMOUNT OF WEIGHT

Advise your partner to turn down foods such as cakes, fatty meat, butter, sweets, puddings and processed foods, to exercise vigorously for half-an-hour a day, and to stick to a calorie intake of around 2000 calories per day for women and 2500 for men. The pounds will fall off.

87.

YOUR PARTNER SPENDS ALL THEIR TIME ON THE INTERNET

Your partner may be having an 'internet affair'. Are they secretive about their activities? Do they insist on a password-protected account on the main domestic computer?

If your partner participates regularly on chat-rooms or forums, they may be masquerading as a Carmelite nun or a Somali pirate, or pretending to have a terminal illness. These sorts of fantasies are all very well – where would novelists be without them? – but the danger is that your partner may come to believe his or her own deceptions.

Encourage your partner to take a week's holiday from the internet and see how they react: most people, on the defensive, will jump at the opportunity to demonstrate they are not dependent on something. You will win either way: if they manage it, they are not as addicted as you thought they were. If they don't manage it, they have publicly demonstrated that they have a problem.

88.

YOUR PARTNER RE-ENACTS WAR TRAUMAS AT NIGHT

Again, see §13. You probably shouldn't be sleeping in the same bed as anyone, and definitely not a trained killer.

A friend of mine's husband regularly strangled, kicked and beat her at night; he was apparently given to dreaming he was a prisoner in a Korean War Red Chinese Re-Education Camp. The strange aspect of it was that he was born in 1972. In therapy sessions he claimed that the dreams were brought on by the fact that his consumer electronics firm was being swamped by Far Eastern imports. The therapist was sympathetic, which slightly surprised my friend, until she discovered that her husband had found the therapist through the Chinese Re-Education Camp Survivors Network. Therapists will tend to act according to their specialisms. As soon as my friend found a proper therapist, her husband was warned that his behaviour was potentially actionable, and it ceased.

If you wish to avoid going this far, there is really only one solution: leave your partner to deal with his Burmese Death-Railway Experience or Norwegian Commando Attack Flashback on his own (I assume that it is a he), and move to the spare room.

Your only other option is to take matters into your own hands and attack him back, waiting until he is peacefully asleep and then ripping out a portion of his hair with an Amazonian war-whoop. This could well cure matters.

89.

YOUR PARTNER TIPS THE KEEPER FAR TOO MUCH AT SHOOTS

Your partner is seeking to prove something: possibly he or she doesn't want to be mistaken for a corporate gun (many of whom won't tip at all), or perhaps that he or she appreciates, more than anyone else, the keeper's work in controlling the beaters in a stiff wind.

The accepted amount for a tip is £20 plus an extra £10 for every 100 birds bagged. Anything more than this is ostentatious. Nor should the money ever be handed over with a flourish. Your partner should fold it up discreetly and pass it to the keeper in a handshake as they accept their complimentary brace of birds.

If the day has been a bad one, or the keeper has been rude or un-
pleasant (shout-
ing 'Here's an easy
one! Even you should be
able to kill this!' for example)
then it is acceptable to withhold a tip,
or ask for a
refund.

90.

YOUR PARTNER INSISTS ON GOING TRICK-OR-TREATING AT HALLOWEEN, DESPITE BEING AN ADULT

Personally I have no particular animus against Halloween, despite it being a transatlantic import. I am all for fancy dress. The fact that nowadays the girls seem to wish to dress as streetwalkers and the boys as blood-spattered zombies is just a cultural phase. At least they are making an effort.

If your partner wishes to join in, despite being in

their 30s, 40s, 50s, etc., there is a problem of potential embarrassment, but it is probably best to let them get it out of their system once a year, even if some elements of cross-dressing are involved. The ease with which most men can be persuaded to dress up as women, in fishnets and bustier, blood-spattered or not, never ceases to amaze me.

What rankles more is an obese uncostumed adult presenting themselves at your door with a buggy in which there is a tiny becostumed baby cradling a bulging bag of treats. The baby, having not yet cut its milk teeth, is unable to consume the sweets, which are obviously for the bulimic mother or father. In these cases further treats should be refused, and a 'trick' asked for instead, which the parent will probably be too corpulent to attempt.

One more general note: if the people who appear are not in costume and/or do not say 'trick or treat', you are entirely justified in withholding their fun-size Mars bar. Gangs of teenagers in hoodies and jeans who show up at midnight and stand there truculently without speaking are not trick-or-treating, but demanding money with menaces.

91.

YOUR PARTNER REGULARLY INSERTS A BLOCK OF KENDAL MINT CAKE INTO THE WASHING MACHINE IN THE BELIEF THAT IT IS DETERGENT

Anyone who is does this is exhibiting absent-mindedness on a level that borders on the dangerous. And what will you feel half-way up Scafell Pike when your partner reaches into their backpack and offers you a soap tablet?

Try talking to your partner about what is preoccupying them. It may be work, or money, or the latest scientific findings about the multiverse. A problem shared is a problem halved (except in the case of the multiverse).

If your partner is unable to remember simple things such as car keys or personal organizers, encourage them to keep a personal organizer to remind them of what they have forgotten. Two personal organizers, or, I suppose, an infinite regression of personal organizers, may be needed here.

92.

YOUR PARTNER'S BREATH SMELLS

Halitosis is extraordinarily easy to cure. It is chiefly caused by food particles trapped in the mouth after eating. Simple brushing of the teeth can cure halitosis at a stroke. While brushing the teeth, your partner should probably also brush their tongue. The trick is to get your partner to brush after every meal or snack, or after consuming beverages such as coffee and alcohol.

After every meal, then, go straight to the bathroom and begin brushing your own teeth. When your partner asks what you are up to, say: 'Apparently it's a fact that brushing after meals gets rid of bad breath. I thought I'd do it to be on the safe side.' Your partner will look worried. If they don't then take the hint, buy them a new toothbrush.

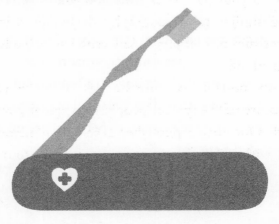

93.

YOUR PARTNER IS ADDICTED TO ROMANTIC FICTION

These books give women unrealistic expectations of men. Not all men have sculpted jaws and locksmiths' fingers and can deliver choreographed and comprehensive deflowerings to swooning dewy-eyelashed heaving-bosomed virgins. Such books are responsible for girls failing to take sensible precautions over their reproductive health, believing that 'surrendering to passion' is more important than forethought. Neither do these books make any mention of nasal hair, monopolizing the television remote control, or unapologetic eructation.

Unfortunately none of this information is very persuasive if your partner is truly addicted. Romantic fiction is similar to pornography or lemon drizzle cake: it satisfies primal urges. Any criticism is likely to be shrugged off.

The only possible way forward is to make your partner aware of the type of people who actually write this stuff. One major publisher I shall not name is supplied with 30% of his entire romantic output by the same man, a white supremacist living in Totnes. Most romantic fiction is written by cynics, many of whom are fat, hideous, chain-smoking men of doubtful personal hygiene; and while writing under names such as Jessica Dawn and Charlotte Devereaux, have real names such as Harold Bong, Clive Winkel and Colin Smith.

Encourage your partner to join the Society of Romantic Novelists (the membership criteria in this age of digital self-publishing are extremely lax) and go to a Society lunch. Your partner will never look at these books in quite the same way again.

94.

YOUR PARTNER LIES

There are five types of lie: a) the whopping lie, b) the white lie, c) the pathological lie, d) the misleading lie, and e) the spiteful lie.

Examples might include a) For security reasons MI5 confiscated the roses I bought you, b) Your new haircut really suits you, c) The thousand-year Reich will be extended to two thousand years as of next Thursday, d) I did a lot of running at Cambridge, and e) During her last hours on earth, I made love to your late wife.

Having said this, lies are an important part of any partnership. How could it be otherwise, when deception is omnipresent in everyday life? We would be shocked if politicians told us the truth; they would become instantly unelectable. Parents lie to protect children from harsh realities concerning the deaths of kittens. Christmas is a time for lies: how else to react to an unwanted gift other than 'It's lovely'? People lie to simplify matters, to protect feelings, to disguise the unacceptable truth; and it is certainly the case that the truth can be as destructive as any lie. Tell your partner that they are occasionally ugly, irritating, dull, passionless and feeble, and you will detonate a crisis from which you may never recover.

In short, if your partner, like everyone else, perpetrates the occasional lie to save your feelings or smooth things over, they should be forgiven. You are often better off with a liar than a saint.

95.

YOUR PARTNER NEVER TAKES THE RUBBISH OUT

This is very simple: don't take it out yourself either. If this book has a lesson, it is that Partner Management must always come before short-term gain. Turn your house into something resembling the Winter of Discontent[8], if necessary. When your partner is forced to take the rubbish out just to clear some space, take the next lot of rubbish out promptly yourself. Repeat the cycle as many times as is necessary.

---

8 For younger readers, the Winter of Discontent was the winter of 1978/9, caused by the Labour government, when there were festering rubbish-mountains in the streets.

96.

YOUR PARTNER PLAYS TABLE TENNIS WITH FRIENDS IN A ROOM HUNG WITH ANCIENT FAMILY PORTRAITS, AND YOU FEAR THE PAINTINGS ARE BEING DAMAGED

In this you are probably quite right: any conservator will tell you that repeated collisions with small fast-moving objects, even if light and air-filled, will abrade the surfaces of delicate artworks, causing paint to flake. If these are truly old and valuable pieces, and especially if they are of your relatives rather than your partner's relatives, and if for some reason the portraits cannot be relocated – for example because there is no space or because your partner wishes to show them off to the business associates with whom they play table-tennis – you have a serious problem.

Fortunately a solution is at hand. Have the paintings copied. There are several reputable firms who will do this for you to a high degree of accuracy using computerized methods, which will include the rendering of *impasto*. Then ship the real paintings off to a bank where they can be kept in storage. Your partner won't be able to tell the difference; indeed, your partner doesn't even need to be informed that you are taking this course of action, if you can keep him or her out of the table-tennis room for a couple of weeks (try arranging it while you are on holiday). Best of all, you will make back the fee for the paintings in your saving on household insurance premiums.

97.

YOUR PARTNER REFUSES TO WEAR FORMAL DRESS

Your partner refuses to wear a suit and tie (if a man) or a dress and shoes (if a woman). The result is that you can't be seen with them at formal occasions. They are not allowed access to the Carlton Club or even a moderately good restaurant.

Tackle the problem at the root. Do they regard the whole of society as rotten and corrupt, and formal dress as a bourgeois affectation, the badge of slavery?

If so, sit them down and ask them what it would really be like to live in a society with no police force, no rule of law, no welfare provision, no health service, no rubbish collection and no pothole maintenance. Probe the resentments that lead them to regard with contempt the judiciary, armed forces and levers of governnment. Were they trampled by a Law Lord as an infant?

Once you have fully addressed these deep-seated aspects of their personality you will be able to attend the opera again.

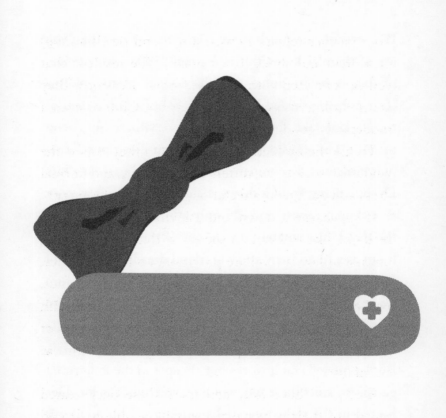

98.

YOUR PARTNER IS FRIGHTENED OF SERVANTS

But servants are much more frightened of you than you are of them! I know this isn't much help, since servito-phobia is as irrational an affliction as pteronophobia (fear of being tickled by feathers) or bufophobia (fear of toads). But take the example of a servitophobic friend of mine. He occasionally lunches at an illustrious Edinburgh merchant's company, and is required to wear a kilt. Despite being from a distinguished family, he is as poor as a church mouse and can only afford to hire a kilt for the day. Unfortunately the design of the sporran marks it out as a hired item, and my friend dreads the sneers of the staff. He came to me for help. My solution for him was to be disarmingly frank. 'Awful, isn't it,' I told him to say as they took his jacket. 'A man at my time of life having to enter the doors of Hector Russell to hire a kilt. But let me tell you it works out cheaper in the long run. I get all my suits there too, white tie and tails, the lot.' Delivered in the right tone of hangdog good humour, this bore the stamp of true aristocracy and endeared him to the staff forever.

99.

YOUR PARTNER IS IMMATURE

Your partner has the emotional range of a panda, i.e. either a) happy or b) sad. They laugh at the word 'poo'. They are unable to leave any wine in a bottle of wine. They spend all their time publishing pictures of their doggie on the internet.

If your partner is a teenager, none of this is very important, but if your partner is older, they need to be given some adult responsibilities. It's possible they have never really suffered; and, after all, it is privation that creates personality.

Your job, therefore, is to make your partner suffer.

I am confident that, having read this far, you are fully capable of doing this.

100.

YOUR PARTNER ALWAYS DOES THE SAME THINGS IN BED

By this I mean: reading; cutting toenails; writing a diary and chuckling; removing make-up; doing tax returns; eating a late sandwich; smoking; sketching; making phone calls and sending texts; counting money into small bags; learning magic tricks; organizing a stamp collection; updating Facebook; learning a foreign language on headphones; meditating (a highly annoying form of silence); playing online Texas Hold 'Em; doing exercises; self-examining for diseases; tatting; assembling Airfix models; practising speeches; attempting a world record; playing the guitar; or assembling jewellery with a small blow-torch.

The only solution (if you insist on sharing a bed in the first place – see §13) is to adopt a zero tolerance policy. A bed is, or should be, a place of peace and tranquillity, not the arena for the 102 things you have forgotten to do that day. The best way to deal with a partner who insists using it as a place to cure hams or practise a golf swing is to enrol them in a class called Discover Your Physical Nibbana. I mention it because such a class has recently started near where I live in Aldershot. Its main thrust is that bed must be a place of ceaseless sexual experimentation. No other activities are permissible, except perhaps sleep. Your partner, after one horrified session (purchased by you as a gift), thinking that this is what you expect from them, will feign sleep as soon as you enter the room, letting their stamp collection fall to the floor with a dull thud.

Discover Your Physical Nibbana can supply gift vouchers.

101.

YOUR PARTNER NEVER REMEMBERS YOUR BIRTHDAY

This is simply remedied: ensure your partner has the latest mobile phone app that will remind them of these important dates. The app can be bought as an inexpensive birthday present (given humorously alongside the real present, of course) or downloaded free.

If your partner still forgets your birthday, despite the fact that their phone has been bleeping and flashing at them continuously for weeks, then there may be a deeper structural reason. Your partner may be a Jehovah's Witness, for example. Have they also been ostentatiously refusing injections?

102.

YOUR PARTNER IS TRYING TO IMPROVE *YOU*

I remember my late mother used to halt all argument with my father by saying: 'You're mistaken, and in any case I am right 85% of the time.' The fact that she had allowed him this generous 15% margin of error, which she somehow managed to convey was only offered as a sop to his pride, and that the figure was disarmingly precise, always sent my father storming impotently out of the room.

Your partner is trying to improve you with the best of motives, even if it is entirely unnecessary. It's quite possible that they love you. So give them the benefit of the doubt. Pretend to go along with their little schemes, despite them being naïve and transparent.

After all, your partner will have little understanding of how *really* to improve their partner (i.e. you) without a copy of this book.

I suggest you keep it well hidden.